BOUNCING BACK from SEPARATION AND DIVORCE

Helping you Untie the Knot and
Benefitting the Family

DREW S. VAN BRUNT MSW.

Trafford
PUBLISHING®

Order this book online at www.trafford.com
or email orders@trafford.com

Most Trafford titles are also available at major online book retailers.

Note for Librarians: A cataloguing record for this book is available from Library
and Archives Canada at www.collectionscanada.ca/amicus/index-e.html

Printed in the United States of America.

ISBN: 978-1-4251-3847-9 (sc)
ISBN: 978-1-4251-3848-6 (e)

*Our mission is to efficiently provide the world's finest, most comprehensive
book publishing service, enabling every author to experience success.
To find out how to publish your book, your way, and have it available
worldwide, visit us online at www.trafford.com*

Trafford rev. 03/14/2011

 www.trafford.com

North America & international
toll-free: 1 888 232 4444 (USA & Canada)
phone: 250 383 6864 ♦ fax: 812 355 4082

Contents

Contents

Introduction

In nineteen-seventy seven, I began working with separated and divorced parents and children. My own journey through divorce of having to cope with emotional, psychological and family issues began in nineteen-eighty four and continued for many years. Many of the ideas presented to you took shape from my personal experience, and have taken form from the thousands of family experiences I have encountered.

Throughout my work, I have offered services to meet the needs of separated and divorced families. A need to resolve parent-teen issues and issues between parents themselves prompted me to seek formal training in conflict resolution. Since the late nineteen-eighties, I have successfully mediated several hundred family agreements. Some scenarios from these mediations are presented to illustrate common themes or issues brought up by couples.

At the same time, despite mediation, it became increasingly apparent that the only means possible for some children to be able to have contact with their parent(s) would be if a social service professional was to oversee their visit. Thus in nineteen-eighty eight, guidelines and procedures were established for supervised access and have since been refined to provide this service. The purpose of supervised access then, as it is today, is to safeguard and ensure the well being of children and to act as a voice for children who want to see and be with their parent(s). The benefits and misuse of Supervised Access will be discussed.

Often as a mediator (and in my current practice as a Separation/Divorce Coach) I have witnessed adults and children struggling to understand and cope with their grief and loss associated with separation and divorce. In order to meet this need I trained and began offering grief coaching during the mid-nineteen nineties. An outline of the process and ways of managing grief will be discussed.

Through working with separated and divorced parents and children I have testified at many custody and access hearings and in numerous family and divorce cases. The Supreme Court of British Columbia, having earned a Masters of Social Work degree specializing in Separation and Divorce, recognizes me as an expert on divorce-related issues such as supervised access. A selection of communication strategies and ideas for use in parenting plans are outlined, highlighting how to avoid critical pitfalls and apply methods that will be of benefit to you, your former partner and your family.

It is in the telling of couples' stories, of parents' stories and the challenges these families and their children present to you that I most wish to acknowledge – it is through sharing their experiences that you can be assisted to 'untie your own knot', and without their stories this book would be incomplete.

These stories and information reveal there is more than just a legal divorce; there are the 'realities' and the 'intangibles' that must also be resolved. The legal divorce, as set out in a court order, outlines a judgment for property (financial matters), custody, access and support. It pronounces an end to the union of your partnership or marriage, divides your family property, says who has physical custody of the children, who will pay and for how long. It also provides people with a false sense of finality that once a court ordered judgment has been made this is the end of the whole matter. As you will find out your reality is about ending one chapter of your life and beginning another, and the process of making this new one work. It is about understanding the process you have or are experiencing, breaking-old habits, finding renewal within, and doing the best with what you have got. It is also about managing and coping with practical matters from financial issues to parenting challenges. It is about finding ways to untie the knot – alleviating feelings of anger, guilt and hurt; letting go of the rope without chaffing your spirit – eliminating feeling of fear, blame and resentment; and, knowing when to hold on, if you have children, to share in parenting responsibilities – to allow for balance and rebuild a sense of family.

One of the greatest difficulties in writing this book centered on what information I should present to parents. After wrestling with presenting parents with such a melancholy outlook I decided to place emphasis on positive parenting practices and include comments from children. Only a few of the most detrimental parenting practices are highlighted and should be avoided.

The chapters of the book are set up, regardless of your current situation, for you to follow in chronological order. You will also notice some steps within chapters and some chapters themselves require you to do exercises that should be reviewed together in order for you to gain a fuller perspective and understanding of your attitudes, beliefs, behaviors or feelings in relation to your separation and divorce. By reviewing the information and working through the questions and tasks you will not only be able to bounce back from the emotional toll and financial impact that comes from divorce, but you will rebound and move to a healthy state in your personal and family life.

The purpose of this book is:

> ▶ To present adults with an overview of the process of separation

and divorce

▶ To provide after separation/divorce ideas and strategies that will allow ex-partners, and or, ex-spouses to best update, refine, or rework existing agreements

▶ To provide adults/parents with means of how to best resolve their separation and divorce that will enable them to move forward with their lives

▶ To provide information, ideas and strategies that will allow parents to become the best parenting partners in raising their children

▶ To offer encouragement, anecdotal information and practical ideas of assistance to parents in creating a nurturing environment for their children

The intention of this book, and that of the author, is not to promote, nor condone divorce, rather to take the position separation and divorce happens, and to make the best of a difficult situation. Having said this, it is vitally important that you take a moment to review the following questions before proceeding: Are you still questioning if you should proceed asking, "Do I want a separation/divorce?" Are you bouncing back and forth between remaining together or not asking questions such as, "Can I make it on my own?", or, "How will I support myself?" Have you clearly thought out the reasons for proceeding with separation/divorce? Have you talked to someone – a counselor, a clergyman, a friend whose opinion you trust, etc. to gain a perspective outside your own? If you do not know the answers to any of these questions precede no further until you have obtained an outside perspective. By doing so, will provide greater insight into what is to be your next step.

You will notice when reading this book, the use of the terms separation and divorce. In our Society today, there seems to be as many people living together as there are people getting married. The numbers of people leaving a partnership in either case also appears to be about the same. However, many people who have left a living-together or common-law relationship consider themselves 'separated' once they are no longer involved in that particular relationship. (In many jurisdictions not all family law is applicable to this type of relationship.) The term 'divorce' is usually used in reference to a person from a break up of a married relationship, however in the book for brevity sake the term 'divorce' is synonymous with 'separation' and will be used in reference to explaining the process an adult or child may experience whether separated or divorced.

Chapter One

Steps to Building a Foundation for Your Healthy Separation/ Divorce

Generally speaking, it takes an average of three to five years for women and five to seven years for men to move through a transition of ending a significant relationship or marriage and recovering from separation/divorce. It can be a process of rough seas with swells and a lot of choppy water before the calm. However, there are positive approaches and constructive strategies that can be planned for and implemented allowing couples, parents and children to positively manage, alleviate stress and cordially end their relationship. For instance, parents can best interact with each other to develop a parenting partnership for the benefit of the 'family'. This is what I call the 'bounce back' effect similar to the rebound of a bouncing ball.

To accomplish this goal you will need to understand the divorce process, be open to looking at your self and be willing to undertake specific tasks to ensure you obtain positive benefits through implementing specific strategies. Having knowledge of the divorce process and strategies to recognize and manage emotions experienced during divorce, you will be able to minimize the hurt, upheaval and stress felt by all 'family members'.

There are many beginnings or starting points to separation and divorce. You may be a person who is contemplating a separation or divorce for the first time, or you may have already begun the process having emotionally separated yourself from your relationship some months or years ago. You may be contemplating physically leaving your relationship/family, or you may have already left. Your partner or spouse may have already emotionally left you, and or, is about to or has physically left you. Whatever your current situation there are questions you first need to answer for yourself, in order to clarify and acknowledge the reasons you have, or will, take action to seek a separation or divorce. Doing so will enable you to move forward and not dwell on the past.

QUESTIONS AND MORE QUESTIONS, THE FIRST STEP
ASK AND ANSWER FOR YOURSELF THE FOLLOWING QUESTIONS:

(You may find writing the answers down on paper or keyboarding the information will help you to focus or gain a clearer picture of your situation. Initially set aside at least an hour, and it may require two or three additional quiet times to complete this exercise. Having the answers on paper will enable you to revisit and add to the ideas you have already outlined.)

▶ What are the reasons I am thinking about, or going to separate or divorce?*

▶ What are the reasons he/she is thinking about, or going to separate or divorce? (Express your thoughts for both these questions above in language like this: "I could not accept the way he/she...", rather than, "He/she did or didn't do this, that, or the other thing." Writing it down in such a way highlights your responsibility in such matters.)

▶ *What* is my *behavior* – action or inaction, thought – said or unsaid and emotion – feelings and attitude that contributed to contemplating or *contributed to your proceeding with separation or divorce?**

▶ *What is their behavior* – action or inaction, *thought* – said or unsaid and emotion - *feelings and attitude that contributed their contemplating or contributed to your proceeding with separation or divorce?*

▶ Then compare how you think you felt about the facts with how you actually reacted, responded, or dealt with them. For example, 'I felt increasingly unhappy not being able to explain what was going on and hurt their (my family's) feelings so I withdrew into my own world.'

▶ What do you expect the outcome of separation/divorce to be? How come?

▶ What does my partner/spouse expect the outcome of separation/divorce to be? How come?

▶ What aspects of separation/divorce are of concern to you? List them.

---

* In each of the above two questions also record how you responded, reacted, and felt about what happened in the relationship. For instance,

'I spent more and more time at the office (away from home) as a way to deal with his/her complaints about the relationship.)

‣ What aspects of separation/divorce are of concern to my partner/spouse? List them.

‣ What do I want the outcome of the separation/divorce to be or look like?

‣ What does my partner/spouse want the outcome of the separation/divorce to be or look like?

‣ From the similarities and differences, how can I make changes to bring about a positive outcome?

‣ From the similarities and differences, how can my partner/spouse make changes to bring about a positive outcome?

‣ What do you envision yourself doing a year, two years, five years after the separation/divorce?

‣ Review this material and take note of what still annoys and upsets you, and affects your current attitudes and behavior.

‣ Put this information aside, re-examine it in a few days, and make adjustments.

The whole point of this exercise is not just self-reflection, but looking at the 'larger' picture. Reflective thinking and feeling leads to reflective listening, and in turn creates effective communication. The better equipped you are recognizing and alleviating your triggers and your ex-partner's the better rapport can be manifested with them. In addition, with respect to parents, the better able you will be in developing a parenting relationship with the other parent.

DEBUNKING COMMONLY HELD IDEAS ABOUT DIVORCE AND FAMILY

Another step towards successfully moving forward with your personal life and your life as a parent is to examine a number of the commonly held myths about divorce and family. Redefining and integrating these ideas into your own beliefs will provide you with a better road map to move past the challenges your separation and divorce will present to you as an adult and further enhance your ability to parent.

From a philosophical perspective your life is in a constant state of change: our body grows, matures, and eventually declines with age; circumstances in our world change – the environment in which we live constantly shifts, the friends you have as an adult are most likely not the friends you grew up with as a child; children you raise or know grow up and become adults; and, how you perceive the world around changes as we interact with the world around us. However, the one constant in life that remains true is change.

So perhaps, it is important for you to examine your belief about your marriage.

Do you carry the notion that you would stay married "Till death do us part", that your marriage would remain life-long? If you do, have you pushed aside or denied problems existed and or pretended all was well so that you did not have to deal with relationship issues that would have changed this notion? If you look at and become aware of your belief regarding marriage and look at the way in which your responses to change have shaped your life you can see how change is linked to growth – you will be able to see divorce as having changed family not ending it; or, the ending of your marriage with children as a beginning of being parenting partners.

Societal assumptions such as: divorce ends the family; divorce ruins children; divorce is abnormal; and, divorce causes your life to run amuck can have a negative impact on how you feel about yourself and cause you to feel overwhelmed and hopeless about your divorce. Here are new assumptions to replace the old that will allow you to envision yourself making positive family changes:

> *Divorce redefines your family* transforming your family into two parental households

> *Children from two parental households can be loved and nurtured as much as children from one household*

> *Divorce occurs as away to undue an untenable situation*

> *The process of divorce is predictable and you can work through the stages*

There are other steps in building a foundation to a healthy separation and divorce. Each step is necessary to be able to implement effective and manageable strategies and plans. You should be working on the next two steps relatively at the same time to receive the maximum benefit of both. Keeping in mind the answers from the first section and the ideas just gathered from the section above will provide you with a focus and reason for performing the tasks outlined in the next step, and possibly in the following step as well. You can also read the fourth section pertaining to the divorce process, the emotional process most people experience to some degree or another, and which is important to be aware of or know what you have, you are or you will most likely experience as a result of the act of separation/divorce itself.

TANGIBLE STUFF YOU NEED TO DO, THE NEXT STEP

If you are moving ahead with this and the following step you are resolute and comfortable moving forward with obtaining a divorce, both in legal terms and in your relationship as well. Here are some initial tasks you must do (Appendix A):

▶ Collect and make copies of bank statements both joint and your partner's or spouse's accounts, including business accounts especially if you believe and feel you have contributed to the business they are operating, *plus tax returns*, loan statements and education expenses. Make copies of at least three years tax returns. These may show depreciation schedules, capital gains and losses (which may identify securities being held) Check to see if your partner has a safety deposit box, if so, record the number and place deposit box is located. If you have a joint safety deposit box take an inventory of what is inside it. Take video or pictures of the contents and have someone be a witness.

▶ If you have been married more than five years, obtain copies of their pension plan contributions by contacting your regional federal branch concerning pensions. In the United States it would be listed as the 401k savings and in Canada it would be listed as Canada Pension Plan (CCP) (If you are also an income earner collect your own information to be prepared in case you are asked for it) Also, collect information on pension monies from employer plans and deferred profit sharing plans. Obtain and gather all information on RRSPs, 401ks, RRIFs.

▶ Copy wills, trust agreements, power of attorney.

▶ If you own property, the residence you live in, and or, other property obtain copies of the terms of sale, purchase agreements, through the broker and or mortgage company.

▶ If you or they, or you have a joint stock portfolio collect financial information on the brokerage account.

▶ Obtain a copy of your partner/spouse's monthly pay stub, or if self-employed a copy of their records, and or, income tax statement that shows yearly earning. If they pay into a benefit's program, obtain a copy of the benefits you receive by contacting the health agency in charge. If you do participate in their plan, and you most likely will lose benefits once the divorce finalizes, calculate the dollar amount you would lose. If you work you will need to collect information on your health insurance, disability, life and property benefits, plus statements if you pay into an annuity.

▶ If you have home insurance make a copy of the policy so that it can be reviewed for possible riders concerning collectibles that form part of your family's assets. Life insurance policy may have a cash-value component built in over time that can be unlocked or used to defer unexpected costs as a result of a changing lifestyle.

- Collect and make copies of bills, invoices, promissory notes payable to or by you, ownership of chattels, etc. on large purchases such as boats, cars, trailers, investments, recreational equipment, including items used for business (keep a separate file for them) – anything over $500 – that is still outstanding or has been paid and shows the full cost of the item.

- If your family has used a computer program such as Quicken or Simply Accounting copy the file to a disk.

- Make a list of all items in the house video or photograph everything: pictures, appliances, jewelry, furniture, cars, recreation equipment, business equipment, kitchenware, accessories, anything of value (including pets). List all assets in your name, theirs or is jointly held – whether they are gifted, inherited, or in the name of a third party on your or their behalf. Include whether the item was acquired prior to or during your marriage. Write down a corresponding replacement value beside each item. Some will be difficult to do and some you may list as priceless because of the sentiment attached to them. On that same list highlight the items that will be difficult to divide for you and items that you believe will be difficult for your partner to divide too.

- List all the monthly expenses (debt) your household incurs (keep bills to show these amounts) such as, food, gasoline, oil or heating, electricity, water or hydro, cable or TV, alarm system, strata fees, sports/recreation or club fees, and any other expenses that contribute to family living (i.e. insurance payments) –use canceled cheques to support claim. Doing this will provide you with an idea of how much monthly income is needed to pay for expenses, in order to be able to survive. Beside each provide reason for each debt. Mark each item you believe expenses can be reduced or eliminated. (These are items when in discussion during mediation or negotiation with your lawyer concerning support that can be adjusted).

- Itemize other payments that may not be monthly i.e. medical and credit card payments. If you are responsible for paying the credit card off consider canceling your account, or reducing the spending limit once you announce your intension to separate or divorce to build your own credit alone. If you have an auxiliary card consider opening your own account to build your credit in advance of separating.

- If you work only part-time, or not at all, make sure you open a separate bank account with a different back to begin to build your own credit. Each week deposit money into this account so that when ready to separate or divorce you have some money to weather through the financial tough times.

▶ Establish your own financial identity by using your credit card and then making payments using the cash to build a credit history. Once you do this for a few months go and apply for a personal line of credit.

▶ Contact the credit bureau and get a copy of your credit report to find out what needs to be improved upon, so you can work on improving your score. This is especially true if you plan to buy or rent a new residence.

▶ If you have a pre- or post-nuptial agreement, make sure you have a copy, since the terms of the agreement may, and often will affect the division of assets

▶ If your assets ($ value of your possessions) total more than $55,000, take a summary of this information to a financial planner. They can discuss ways of how best to spit your assets and financially manage them after the separation/divorce. (This will provide you with a good idea about how to divide major assets, but may not include what some jurisdictions, states and provinces set as minimum standards for child support.)

▶ If you work part-time, or is a parent that left a job, ended a career, or disrupted university or other training to raise children and manage the home you need to do the following:

1. Write down your entire daily tasks, and then categorize them into themes i.e. housekeeping (laundry, dusting, vacuuming, making beds, etc.), cooking (making meals, lunches etc.) grocery shopping, chores outside home (banking, pay bills, dry cleaning, etc.). If you keep track of the monthly expenses, add a section for record keeping and add any other tasks you do to the bottom of this list. Then place beside each item, breaking down to the nearest quarter hour, the time you spend on each activity i.e. /day, /week, /month.

2. If you are approximately under the age of 45 years, you need to investigate the job market. If you had a job or career go to a career/employment counselor in your area and ask them on information/statistics regarding the rise in level of income and skill set that the average person in your original position would be working at today. Also, find out what education, training and cost would be required to reach this level. If you were in university or training institute, or had just completed university or training there are statistics that indicate what earning level you would be making today. You can use a sum of money in your financial settlement for retraining or getting your career back on track. This will help bolster your self-esteem and help you focus on the future.

3. If you are approximately over the age of 45 years you need to do the same as in section #2 above, however, depending on the job or career you were in before some of these positions/careers may not be possible to return to due to age, and or, retraining requirements. If you believe this to be the case, calculate in addition to present earning level of the position you left or work part-time, and find out about future earnings of this position to age 65 years.

4. While still in the marriage or partnership make sure all material items are in working order, are repaired, or replaced in the home by taking full advantage of your home insurance coverage. Also, take full advantage of your family insurance by having dental work done, eyes checked, eyeglasses fixed/replaced and medical needs met. Make sure your children are up-to-date on their dental, medical and other health-related visits. Begin to build an inventory by gathering extra cleaning supplies, new shoes, extra clothes for the children so you can reduce your costs once you are on your own. (The reason for gathering information for #2 and #3 is that the longer you have been married and supporting your family by raising children and maintaining your household the better the weight given for your future support, whether through mediation or the courts.)

- If you decide to choose seeking a divorce or separation I would also suggest you visit your local library, law court library or university/college library to review the divorce laws and laws regarding a legal separation in your state or province. Each state can, and frequently does, treat marital circumstances and living together partnerships in different ways. In Canada, a federal divorce law applies to all provinces, however each province has a different family relations act and different circumstances for living together partnerships. Having an insight into the law in your state or province will better prepare you to ask questions and understand the answers a lawyer will give you in regard to your situation, and allow you to gain a better understanding of how your matter will be procedurally handled in court.

- Think about where you are going to live if you are planning on moving out. Decide where you are going to live and figure out how much it will cost by looking in real estate ads or magazines to learn about rent or cost of purchasing an apartment or home. Also, remember to factor in the costs of moving, set-up costs i.e. telephone and utilities.

What happens if the other person leaves first? Is doing this tangible stuff applicable? Yes, including a few more steps to allow you to focus and move beyond the initial stage of *shock*.

▶ Talk to your 'Ex' to see if there is common ground for you to go to a mediator or lawyer. If they are unwilling to talk to you or they are resistive to discussing anything to do with settling your relationship then seek professional advice from a family law lawyer.

▶ It is important to find out about finances, so go back to the last section and do everything concerning money issues.

▶ In order to move beyond shock, feeling devastated, or feeling angry seek assistance to deal with your emotions – a counselor, divorce coach, etc. Do this to take care of your self emotionally.

▶ Take up a new activity and be open to new ideas.

▶ Remember the comment below. You are the only one who knows how you feel. Give yourself time to deal with your feelings and with the tangibles.

There is no set timetable to complete these tasks. You may find receiving copies of pension or mortgage information somewhat frustrating, as you may have to contact individuals a few times to direct and focus them onto getting you this information. Be persistent and patient, as it may take as long as six to eight weeks to get what you want. Continue to work on gathering information and copies of materials as you proceed with the next step.

If you plan on receiving support – whether for yourself or your children then make sure you do look closely at your possible financial situation before you negotiate your separation agreement, because in some states and in Canada there are rules for how spousal and child support are taxed. For instance, spousal support is deductible for the payer, and is included in the income of the payee, as long as the recipient is receiving support as written in the separation agreement or court order, and those payments are made on a periodic basis. Check with Revenue Canada or state laws concerning specific details applicable to your situation. Also, make sure when you divorce, any benefit to your former spouse under your will is automatically revoked. However, this does not apply to areas you have designated them as your beneficiary such as RRSPs in Canada and K401s in the U.S., insurance, and the like. You have to do that yourself. If your will includes them as Power of Attorney for your financial or personal care make sure to remove them, including executing trade orders on your behalf if you have a brokerage account.

MORE SELF-REFLECTION, ANOTHER STEP

The process of Divorce is like an iceberg, most of it hidden beneath the surface. So in order to size up and better recognize the dimensions of your divorce you will need to go scuba diving of a sort – using your own Self-contained Understanding of Bias and Affect. By examining the ways you act, react and respond to your feelings and thoughts will give you fresh insight about yourself – doing so will enable you to act consciously and take responsibility for your actions rather than behaving in an automatic way or style of response. This is important because it will effect how you interact with others on a daily basis and it is important to your self so that you can build not only a healthy divorce, but ever mindfully move forward with your life.

Nurturing your own self-image is also important in being able to better transmit healthier messages you give your children that form the basis of their own self-image. For instance, if you have a stressful job and you silently worry about how successful you are doing in your work, and you do not discuss or explain these worries quite often you may be projecting your anxiety by being impatient with your partner or family. You may not even realize how often you are like this or that your behavior links to your work anxiety. The cycle works like this: you come home feeling anxious, you don't respond cheerfully or with exuberance to your partner's, and or, child's greeting, instead you respond with a muted reply feeling you want peace and quite and appear disinterested in everyone. Of course, this is not what you want everyone to think and feel, however you have given them that message.

By being aware of your state of mind and attitude you can visualize what may occur if you project this state of mind onto others, thus you can be responsible for your interactions with others. Understanding how your emotions, behavior, and or, body language drive communications can enhance your effectiveness to interact with people. It gives you the option to make changes.

The more you recognize and understand of your self the more ready and able you are to work through and recover from losses and experience joy. The greater your ability to express sadness, loss, anxiety, anger, etc. the better able you will be to work through these and other feelings sooner. Recognizing and understanding how a feeling manifests itself does not mean succumbing to it. Rather, the more you are aware of your emotions the less you will be driven by them, and the more authentic and masterful at empowering yourself you will be.

To assist you with self-reflection here is a self-test on your self-image: (Be open about your thoughts – you may surprise yourself.)

> ▶ How do you see or envision yourself? What are your strengths, areas needing improvement and neutral characteristics?

▶ How do you think/feel other people usually think/feel about you as a person? Would these people describe you as someone they know little about you, or would they describe you as a character from a movie?

▶ What characteristics do you have that you like them to see? And, in what setting would you like to see you using these characteristics?

▶ Further to the last question – how would you like people to see you?

▶ How do you really feel about yourself?

▶ Looking at the positives and negatives, describe what the 'real' you is.

▶ How do you express your 'real' or authentic self? Are you for example: dominate, out-going, passive, quiet, organized, cluttered, social, avoid people, express anger, suppress anger, active, inactive, happy, moody, optimist, pessimist, complains or finds something positive to say, and so on.

▶ How do you deal with occasions when you reveal a side of yourself you would rather not expose?

FURTHER QUESTIONS FOR PARENTS:

▶ What was the reason you wanted children prior to them being born?

▶ What role did you envision yourself being to your children?

▶ What role did your children expect?

▶ How did having children meet your expectations?

▶ Is your role after divorce what you want? If not, what needs to happen to make your role a reality? (Answer this question by talking about your self i.e. 'I need to...', or, 'We need to...' if it is a joint parenting task, instead of 'If they did this I could do that'.)

▶ What are your children's expectations of your role as a parent?

You may find inconsistencies in your answers – this is o.k. What this shows is that you reveal yourself according to the desired image you want to present at the time.

The purpose of the exercise is to further your understanding of knowing your characteristics – your feelings, thoughts, attitudes and behaviors that contribute to who you are, so that you can effectively work on yourself. The more often you self reflect the seemingly easier it will become; the more consistent your authentic self will appear to be; and, the more changes can effectively be made.

At this point, you should have gained a more concise and clear understanding of your life situation from answering questions in the first section. You should have or be completing the 'tangible stuff' needed to support your decision, and show through information you have collected your monetary worth inside and outside your relationship. Finally, you should have and should continue through self-reflection look at how you 'operate' to better understand the way you interact with people in order to be able to make effective and positive changes in responding to people.

THE DIVORCE PROCESS, THE EMOTIONAL EXPERIENCE

Research and theory on the emotional process and stages individuals experience during divorce all seem to have common themes, yet vary in terminology and in the number of stages discussed. The following explanation of two commonly held ideas will provide you with an understanding of the emotional experience most of you will encounter.

Constance R. Ahrons, PhD., in her book, 'The Good Divorce', describes five transitions of divorce: the decision; the announcement; the separation; the formal divorce; and, the aftermath. These transitions[1] are turning points. For many adults and children they can be uncomfortable moments signifying the end of something familiar and the beginning of something new. Transitions are times you can choose to anticipate with anxiousness, forbearing and vulnerability or you may choose to approach them as opportunities for personal growth.

As she describes, the most disruptive part of the process occurs during the first three transitions, namely when an individual decides to divorce, the open disclosure to their partner/spouse and your family and the physical act of leaving the relationship. During these particular periods, adults may feel out of control experiencing stress, moods of ambivalence and ambiguity and times of questioning and internal, as well as external conflict or power struggles. Parents' experiences will be even more complex and difficult in trying to sort out matters concerning their children.

The fourth transition of the process, the formal divorce, refers to terminating the relationship through mediation, and or, by legal means and can be as emotionally disruptive as the previous transitions if matters are left unresolved from these previous periods.

The aftermath, the fifth or last transition, refers to a state in which individuals deal with unresolved family and relationship issues stemming from their previous relationships. As Ahron states, "[the aftermath] infuses life for many years...well after the legal divorce is completed".[2]

---

[1] Constance R. Ahrons. The Good Divorce P. 75
[2] Constance R. Ahrons. The Good Divorce P. 77

Take note that these transitions progress one to the other and tend to overlap. This phenomenon is often brought up in comments made by separated couples and divorcees, who also reveal that during the first three transitions, each partner or spouse take on one of two distinct roles – the initiator or the recipient. The initiator is the person who initiates the decision to divorce and often emotionally distances him or herself from the relationship before physically leaving. During the first transition, the recipient often feels uncertain, initially unaware of their partner's distancing, and as the transition progresses, by their partner's shift away from participating in their relationship. Next, when the initiator discloses their intent to seek a divorce the uncertainty felt by the recipient abruptly changes to a state of shock or numbness upon learning of the decision to divorce, and then changes to denial, anger, hurt, pain, and disbelief as the announcement becomes more real.

Paul and June had been married for ten years. The first few years of their relationship were very happy, but as both their jobs began to put more and more demands on them, as each advanced in their careers, they found themselves spending less and less time together. Every weeknight and weekend became the occasional weeknight and weekends, which then became most weekends, and then regressed to occasional weekends or one weekend day a week. While June had some extra time off for vacation, she realized 'both she and Paul were like two ships in the night'. She was aware of Paul but did not have much of a connection with him. When they were together, she recognized they merely behaved and said things on automatic. They seemed more like roommates than anything else. So, she tried reconnecting and Paul made an effort too, but their schedules quickly forced them into the same routine. June decided next with her spare time to do a number of activities she had wanted to try, but after a few months realized this would not replace her relationship, but knew, their relationship was at an end. For several months she fretted and agonized about making the decision to divorce Paul. Paul sensed something was 'not right' but continued on not discussing this with June, as he was not sure if the pressure caused it from work. One Friday evening, a month or so before their eleventh anniversary, during a rare evening together, June announced to Paul she wanted a divorce. Initially, Paul seemed calm and ok with divorcing June, agreeing with thoughts as to why she felt this was best for both she and Paul. However, within days, having had time to think about it, his feeling of disbelief became anger with the thought of having put so much time into their relationship. How could she throw it all the way, he thought? Sometime later, having gone through the other transitions and emotional process Paul realized this was best for both of them.

Andrew had been considering ending his relationship to Helen for nearly six months. They had been married for eight years and had two children, ages six and eight. Like the previous couple, Andrew and Helen's relationship had slowly drifted apart and remained connected through maintaining 'routine', focused in this case on family matters. "Parenting of their children", as he put it, "is the only positive thing left in their relationship." They either got into an argument, or did not speak about other things. On an evening prior to the children going to their friend's home for the weekend, Andrew and Helen had a heated discussion and Andrew decided that enough was enough and told Helen they would conclude their discussion on the weekend when the children were gone. That weekend Andrew told Helen of his decision to get a divorce. Helen's immediate reaction was one of shock but quickly changed to resolute calm agreeing with Andrew, as she had figured this was the inevitable course given the state of their relationship. I was contacted by Andrew and spoke to both of them regarding arranging a parenting plan. However, upon hearing of how they arrived at their current situation I asked each of them if they had gone to a counselor to discuss and possibly resolve their communication issues before ending their relationship in divorce. They had not gone to a counselor, and felt they should do this before taking the final step. Counseling resulted in healthier ways of communicating with each but they mutually felt their relationship was 'loveless' between themselves and full of 'love' for their children.

Part of the 'announcement' transition is disclosure to family and close friends that you are seeking a divorce. In the case of Helen and Andrew, both were encouraged to be present, as a show of support, while one person spoke to their children regarding their divorce (see sharing parenting section). They planned what to say and thought simple was best; felt they needed to mention and emphasize to their children that both parents love and would continue to love and be their for their children; and, believed they needed to also encourage their children to approach them if they had any concerns or questions. Both Andrew and Helen spoke to their parents and their close friends to minimize embarrassment, so if someone found out – and people do – it was on their terms and not a surprise. If you are able, mutually agree upon whether it is best to disclose your separation or divorce separately or together to each other's parents and friends, and set a timeframe. As clarifying the situation avoids misunderstanding from others and helps you accept the situation, allowing you to get on with moving through your divorce and the emotional process.

Be prepared that friendships between your friends and business colleagues and theirs, relationships with your family and your in-laws and other family members and relations may change for the short-term or irreparably change all together.

The saying 'you never know who your friends are until tough times' can apply to your experience of separation and divorce. You often will not know how friends and others will react to your separation/divorce until you are experiencing it. However as stated, disclosure of the breakup of your relationship avoids having to anticipate embarrassing and problematic situations in the future for you and frees yourself to spend your energy and time moving forward with your life. Speaking with close friends about it may not prevent the shock, withdrawal, resentment, or the loss of support they may show. Be aware, your divorce can devastate some friendships and can strengthen others. Some of my closet friendships were torn apart not just because they cared and had feelings for both of us as a couple, but because of their own expectations of what marriage, being in a relationship meant to them – and we, I, no longer fit that criteria. I became a single amongst the couples.

For recipients the struggle deciding to divorce begins the moment of the initiator's announcement. At the same time, the recipient now begins an emotional state of catch up experiencing similar emotions of those the initiator originally felt at the beginning of their process. This is why, I believe, often as in contentious family matters, you will hear one party saying of the other, "They are not on the same page." The initiator is often the person who has had time to reflect upon the emotions experienced during the first two or three transitions, whereas the recipient has not. It is also a reason that couples and parents who begin and move through the fourth transition, 'the formal divorce' have a difficult time satisfactorily resolving their divorce issues by court proceedings. In such cases, mediation for some couples allows them to discuss and resolve emotional impasses that set the groundwork for dealing with other family issues.

While moving from and through one transition to the next, a tide of emotional states can rush in and around you. These states correspond to the stages espoused by Elisabeth Kubler-Ross[3], M.D., what a person experiences due to the death or loss of a loved one – a mourning process. In your case, it is the death of your relationship and the states you will experience can occur chronologically, may occur in any order and with any combination of states, and can be experienced during any of the first four transitions. As you recognize, understand and deal with the emotions of each state the impact of them on your daily life becomes minimal.

Here are the names of many of the emotions experienced during this process:

Anger; Denial; Shock; Uncertainty; Sadness; Frustration; Resentment; Bitterness; Fear; Insecurity; Jealousy; Guilt; Hatred; Despair; Loneliness; Anxiety; Self-pity; Self-hate; sense of Failure; Desperation; Rejection, Loss of Control; feeling Overwhelmed; and, Grief.

No matter your personal circumstances surrounding the relationship/marriage breakdown, certain states have a healing effect on emotions. A number of factors interplay with being able to move forward through the process. First, the better your understanding of your experience and the feelings associated with it, you

---

[3] *Elisabeth Kubler-Ross M.D., Death & Dying. 1997*

stand a greater chance of being able to move beyond your separation and divorce. Second, how you face the emotional pain regarding the loss of your relationship will greatly influence the efficiency of your healing process. If you try to ignore the pain, it endures and becomes an annoyance, a bother that you keep encountering without your control. If however, you recognize, understand and deal with the feelings of being hurt as they surface you are able to cope in the moment and not let these feelings disrupt your daily life. Next, the person leaving the relationship often experiences the mourning process differently, as the decision and thoughts to withdraw from the relationship have already been worked through, whereas the other partner or spouse must deal initially with shock when upon disclosure. Separation shock is the actual numbing effect of the marriage or relationship has ended and wrestling with accepting the fact the relationship is indeed over.

Finally, the shock that the separation produces is in direct proportion to the part your relationship has played in shaping one's identity. If a person's role is linked and associated to their relationship, often their self-image will be greatly altered once disclosure to separate occurs.

The acronym for these states is termed DABDA and D stands for *denial,* A is for *anger,* B for *bargaining,* D is for *depression* and A for *acceptance.*

Denial occurs when a partner or spouse acts or takes the attitude of denying something exists or is true. It is to behave and act in state of disbelief by pushing away what has or is currently happening, and or, to not accept what is said or done by your partner or spouse and continue to live status quo.[4]

In Paul and June's case, June had been emotionally distancing herself from Paul for sometime. Paul questioned June about her behavior and she openly brought to Paul's attention issues that had in her opinion be going on and needed to be changed. Paul listened, but could not believe matters were that serious. He believed issues between them were due to the stress she felt working long hours. Daily life continued without change and Paul continued to believe happenings in their life was due to 'outside stuff', as he called it and it would pass.

Loni and Ken both had demanding jobs and work commitments had tested their relationship. However, after the birth of their daughter Zoe they each felt that raising their child together would bring them closer having to be parents. Once maternity/paternity leave ended, each took different work schedules to be able to care for Zoe. Unfortunately, their relationship waned and by the time Zoe was a year old Loni and Ken were divorced. Each felt the loss of their relationship, the loss of expectations they had for the each other and each felt hurt by having to

---

[4] *Terms used to express people who are in a state of **denial** are: pushing away; disbelief; not accepting of; not in the right mindset; not in true frame of mind*

endure comments made by the other. Both did not recognize the other as being a positive parent, and only choose to recall what they each had done to care for Zoe. As such, each parent sought sole custody. It was not until their attitude for one another changed, did an amiable solution come about emphasizing the best interests of Zoe.

Denial is a state that can link to other emotions, as mentioned above, such as being hurt. It can also link to emotions such as blame, as presented in this next story. After the divorce, Steven continued to believe Beth was solely responsible for the demise of their marriage. He also saw her as having disrupted his relationship with their children, and blamed her for his poor relationship with them. It seemed evident to everyone who knew Steven that he dismissed and refused to accept the truth of his situation. As a result, his state of denial was associated with another state, that of anger.

Anger is a state of feeling or acting out displeasure. It can be a feeling of being upset, or as mentioned be associated with blame. It is a state closely linked with *denial.*

When Paul finally recognized his relationship was nearing the end his *denial* quickly changed to *anger,* as he felt helpless or powerless to change it. *Anger* in Steven's case occurred after the divorce, but like the other four states can occur anytime during the divorce process. It can occur anytime a person finds himself thinking about, recalling or reliving an event that sparks an emotion of displeasure. Anger can occur when the other has hurt a partner, when a partner/spouse changes behavior leads to confusion and miscommunication.

Often during the set up of access visits, I witness one or both parents express anger at having to relive their past relationship and connect with a former partner or spouse, whom they are trying to distance both physically and mentally in their life. While discussing access arrangements with Traci, a mother of a three year old boy named Blake, I listened to her describe her frustration regarding the dynamics of her relationship with her former partner Chris. This emotion quickly changed to anger as she relived all the difficulties she said she had to endure. After listening to her, I asked her to describe Chris' parenting. She said he was a excellent father, but she was concerned about his inconsistency in seeing Blake indicating it had been a few months since he last saw Blake, and prior to that he had seen Blake off and on once, sometimes twice per week. When I meet with Chris his frustration was apparent almost immediately for having to have supervised access (visits), and he was angry with Traci for not allowing him to see Blake regularly ' without having to go through a grand production', as he called it. Chris also described his relationship with Traci as difficult, but also said she was an excellent parent. A supervised access agreement was set up to commence and continue on a regularly scheduled day and time each week. After a couple of weeks of access being so positive for everyone, it was increased to twice per week. As is often the circumstance, after a set period of time and set number of access visits has occurred the matter returns to court to deal with whether supervised access should continue or not. However, Traci and Chris choose to voluntarily end supervised access recognizing Chris' ability to parent and interact with Blake was positive and were able to arrange a consistent and mutually agreed upon access schedule. The anger both felt towards one another subsided and they were able to communicate about parenting via e-mail.[5]

At first, Andrew pushed away thoughts his marriage was ending and believed Heather would continue with their relationship. However, frustration replaced these thoughts when he tried and was unable to talk to her. After moments like this, he would end these attempts feeling angry and wonder off muttering, or he would leave the house and curse into the wind while getting into his car and driving off.

He decided to change his behavior believing that she would respond. She did at first, but quickly countered his behavior as she was unsure what his intentions were and she felt vulnerable. Andrew's behavior is one example of the state of bargaining.

Bargaining is a state of belief and action that occurs to minimize, eliminate or enhance the circumstances currently existing in a relationship in order to stabilize or bring about status quo. It can be a belief that if the other person in the relationship did some action or stopped doing a certain behavior the relationship would return to 'normal'. It can also be a belief that if you take some action, as in Andrew's case, or if you stop doing some action or behavior the relationship would remain as usual. The partner/spouse is not trying to stop or take some action because he or she is satisfied with the relationship, but done for some other motive. They may feel guilty over separating/divorcing and will say anything or try to take action to make the situation disappear. Unfortunately, their words, and or actions, are often unrealistic and both people realize the suggestions or actions were for the wrong reasons. Ultimately, the situation starts all over again.

Lisa and Ron had been married for more than thirty years. Their relationship had both ups and downs. They were parents of two wonderful adult children. Lisa had supported Ron with his career having stayed home when the children were young and continued to look after the home affairs once the children were in school. They were now an empty nest couple and Ron was nearing retirement. However, the couple's relationship with each other was loveless. Lisa felt the relationship was empty and she felt restless wanting a sense of purpose in her life. She believed

---

[5] For more detail see the section on supervised access

while she was in good health and sound mind that it was best for her to leave, travel and do things she wanted to do – take courses, learn hobbies, meet people and visit different cultures. Ron could not believe their relationship was at an end, and at first carried on as if nothing was different, while Lisa continued making plans to leave. Ron soon began to bargain with her, saying that if she wanted to travel he would travel with her, and that he would support her taking classes, doing crafts, etc. by looking after the house. The thought of being alone and lure of being in a relationship felt comfortable and appealed to her, so she stopped making plans to leave and remained with him. However, she remained restless and their relationship remained loveless.

The luster of being comforted by familiar circumstances soon tarnished and within a month she found an apartment. Within a couple of months, they had reached an agreement concerning the division of assets and Lisa began traveling. Once Ron's attempt at bargaining failed his feeling changed to anger blaming Lisa for the demise of their relationship. Shortly after Lisa physically left the home, Ron seemed to become listless, did little work, let his appearance slip wearing only comfortable clothing and had contact with very few people other than his children. Ron was experiencing the state of *depression* known as feeling blue; in a funk; down; feeling lousy; discouraged; powerless; in despair; and or, having a sense of loss. It is not the clinical kind, but if a person's circumstances intensified and went unchecked for more than a month, their mental health should be brought to the attention of a physician.

Ron continued to find he would bounce between several states of *denial, anger, bargaining* and *depression* within a few days – even within a day. He often found himself thinking of ways he could make concessions to woo Lisa into continuing their relationship. As the cycles recurred, especially *bargaining,* Ron spent less and less time attending to his business and other matters. He was experiencing reactive depression having lost hope he would reunite with Lisa – equivalent to a car being stuck in neutral. With support from his adult children and a counselor Ron changed *reactive depression* into *proactive depression.* In a p*roactive depression* state a person like Ron instead of allowing the other states to recur and feel overwhelmed by the process, they begin to look at and find ways to deal with bettering their circumstances – equivalent to shifting into gear. The difference between *reactive* and *proactive depression* is that a person realizes or senses the marriage is *over.* This is when a person realizes a big piece of their past is slipping away, expectations are lost and the future seems to be full of uncertainty. For Ron, once he accepted the relationship was over there was no need to *bargain,* and as he gradually took responsibility for his behavior in the relationship, his anger waned. As he took more positive and proactive steps his sense of being overwhelmed faded and he was no longer feeling powerless. He moved through the *depression* state.

The final letter in the acronym DABDA refers to the state *Acceptance*. It is a conditional and progressive state. That is, the more proactive a person deals with the other states the less impact these states have on your daily life. *Acceptance is* an attitude reconciling the issues between your former partner/spouse's needs to end the relationship and these issues no longer impacting on their daily life.

In Ron's circumstance, once he began and continued to gain a fuller perspective as to how his relationship ended with Lisa, the less upset and discouraged he became and the less reminiscing he did of things he could do or should have done to make the relationship work. The result, each state recurred less often and with less intensity having less and less affect upon his daily life. For Ron, this meant he certainly found himself at times drifting back into various states, but he did not stay or dwell long in any state. The more he can 'stand in the present' and not dwell on the end of his relationship the more he has been able to move forward in his life.

If your relationship with your former partner or spouse continues in the form of being parenting partners, you will be able to handle this relationship without any hidden or resentful feelings once you reach acceptance, the letting go of the attachment to the former relationship. Have an understanding of the emotional process will better equip you to implement a plan to obtain a separation or divorce. Knowing and taking steps to minimize or eliminate these stages will enable you to develop and proceed along a course of action you will feel comfortable and assured in order to successfully obtain separation or divorce. The next chapter discusses the various ways to implement a plan.

Chapter Two

Implementing Your Plan – Building Your Team

Regardless of how amiable your separation and divorce seems to be, whether you have children or not, or how intricate your financial situation may or may not be you should seek the assistance of friends, family members, and or, professionals to guide you through some or all of the legal, emotional/psychological, personal and family issues. However many of you, like many couples have done, may choose to end their relationship and separate, or end their marriage and divorce without seeking legal counsel, financial advice, separation/divorce coaching, grief counseling or support from friends/family. Consider from a practical perspective, the end of your relationship as the dissolution of a business arrangement. If you were ending a business partnership, wouldn't you seek out legal as well as financial advice to ensure you would obtain the best possible outcome? And, from a personal perspective, in order to be able to deal with the emotions of ending a partnership, and coming to some form of acceptance regarding the loss of your dreams, hopes and expectations as a couple, wouldn't you seek out the help. Seek out the support of friends/family and professionals to gain a fuller understanding of what you are about to, have, and will experience. Consider this in relation to something as simple as trying on clothes, we ask other's opinion of how we look to gain a fuller opinion. So on matters concerning one's mental and psychological health should it not be important to gain a fuller understanding about ourselves in order to be able to make decisions that are more informed for our family and ourselves?

(Note: For couples that are living 'common-law' please also see chapter 7 the section entitled *Non-Traditional Families*.)

Having said this, there are those of you who will still seek to separate and divorce by means of the so-called do-it-yourself-divorce kits*. Such kits are available and used in most jurisdictions. These kits are marketed to divorcing people as an easy means of avoiding lawyers and paying their legal fees. Do not risk the do-it-yourself route if you have to resolve issues such as division of property and other assets, and or, need to resolve matters concerning children and parenting issues.

If you plan to use the do-it-yourself-divorce kits both you and your spouse must be on reasonable speaking terms to be able to reach an agreement, otherwise you will probably be seeking out the services of a mediator or lawyer. Criteria for using these kits include: you and your spouse do not have children – no child support; you and your spouse have been married for less than five years – little or no transfer of pension monies to discuss; you and your spouse each have a combined net worth of less than $50,000 – little or no complex financial matters to worry about; and, you are both currently employed and are each capable of supporting yourself outside the marriage – no spousal support. You will have to take your documentation in person to have a Notary (see section on lawyer/notary below) sign and swear your information for acceptance by the Court. If your situation does not fit these criteria then consider choosing another alternative to obtaining a divorce.

The following sections look at each team member and their function each can provide to assist you in obtaining your separation/divorce. Gaining an understanding of who the team players are will help you identify how you should proceed and in what way is best for you and your family to obtain the separation/divorce – the process discussed in the last section of this chapter.

N.B. Criteria for *selecting members of your team:*

People often hire professionals based on a referral or recommendation from a friend or trusted colleague. However, only use the recommendation as an endorsement to seek an interview with this professional. It should not be the only consideration for hiring them. Remember the person who referred and hired them did so because they met their needs and may not necessarily meet your needs. Hire a professional only when you are comfortable and confident they are aware of your needs; you believe and feel confident they will provide you with solid advise; and, you believe and feel they are capable of assisting you to address your issues and family needs.

If not, seek out another professional who fits these criteria. Finally, choose two or three individuals to interview. The time and energy spent by you in doing so, provides you with a truer perspective as to what service providers offer in your community.

Here are number of ways to obtain a legal Separation/Divorce:

- Do-it-yourself divorce kits/Notary/Application to Court (see * above)

- Mediation (Other professionals – Ops) /Lawyer/Application to Court

- Lawyer (Ops)/Divorce Coach/Application to Court

- Divorce Coach (Ops)/Mediation/Lawyer/Application to Court

- Divorce Coach/Lawyer (Ops)/Application to Court

TEAM MEMBERS YOU MAY SELECT ARE:

YOURSELF; Family Mediator; Lawyer (Notary); Divorce Coach; other social service professionals; Financial Advisor; Real Estate Appraiser; and, Realtor.

YOU, YOURSELF (former partner and family)

To achieve a physical and legal separation/divorce will require you to spend a lot of time, energy, thought and emotion to organize, implement and follow through with a plan. YOU have to know your needs, think of your ex's needs, and the needs of your family to arrive at the best and most suitable parenting strategy, and be able to reach a fair and equitable division of assets. Included in this section is also a review of some of the most common pitfalls newly separated people need to avoid while going through the process of a divorce.

It is common for newly separated people, during the first year of being on their own again, to entangle themselves in one of these pitfalls. If your recognize yourself in any of these situations you have already been involved in one of these situations – do not be alarmed, doing so is quite normal. In moderation, none of these behaviors should cause havoc. However, when done in excess they can do serious harm to you and your family, both emotionally and psychologically.

- Work as Avoidance – To escape the feelings associated with separation a person buries themselves into their job or career, to avoid the loneliness of going home to an "empty" place, which causes them to think about and feel emotions they do not want to experience. The longer you avoid dealing with these thoughts and feelings the more you rob yourself of fully being able to experience other things in life and remain stuck.

- The Rebound Relationship – It is very easy with your emotions moving all over the spectrum that a person finds themselves "falling in love" with the first person who seems nice and takes an interest in them – someone who offers affection, a sympathetic ear, and willingly wants to spend time with you. Most often, the rebound relationship provides temporary comfort in meeting needs but do not usually last because the needs remain unfulfilled. It is natural to feel drawn toward the first, or one of the first caring and nurturing people you meet. As time goes by, and you are able to manage meeting more and more of your own needs the rebound relationship often appears a lot different than when it began. The problem then becomes you now have to contend not only with your divorce, but also with another breakup of this new relationship. Feelings of guilt may occur because you have rejected and hurt another person, and if you have children, for causing further confusion about someone else leaving their life, the children had developed a relationship with them.

- Being Involved With Someone Inappropriate – Sometimes those people who we already are acquainted with become our rebound relationship, such as your boss, child's teacher, friend's partner, or siblings partner, etc. Getting involved with anyone like this will cause problems. Friendly or cordial relationships become strained and awkward once the, as in most instances, brief affair ends. Relationships with other half's partner often becomes very strained and can lead to avoidance or cessation of the relationship altogether.

- Sleeping Around – for some recently separated people having sex with a multitude of people is a way of satisfying a powerful drive – it feels better than sleeping alone, and also a way to overcome feeling a sense of loneliness. When a person sleeps with someone to avoid sleeping alone, in order not to feel lonely, sex becomes an escape, to avoid the feelings that arise when you are single – having to deal with your self by yourself, not with the support of some else.

- Withdrawal or Shutting out the World – Another common response in dealing with separation shortly after it occurs is to withdraw from human contact, and to shut down from the emotional pain associated with it. Some people do so to avoid the embarrassment of having to tell people – guess what most people will know within a few months anyway, so it is best to deal with it so you can move on faster and further from that event.

- Denial or Carrying On As If It Never Happened – just like the reason above people try to carry on as if nothing happened because they do not want to deal with the pain associated with being separated. They deny "the existence" of being separated because they fear having to change and fear of the unknown. The key to dealing with this situation is accepting the fact that being on your own is very different from being married.

- Returning Home to Your Parents – A pitfall, occurring amongst separated people in their twenties and in their mid-fifties and older, is to move back in with their parents. The appeal is the sense of family and security of feeling comfortable, nurtured and cared for. This is usually a short-term remedy, as adults who return home find their status reverted to when they were a child. Moving home and remaining there too long will undermine your chances for reforming your adult identity for yourself.

- Excessive Drug or Alcohol Use – Abusing drugs and alcohol before and after separation is quite common, as many people are emotionally susceptible and vulnerable to drug and alcohol use at this time. Doing so eases the pain and numbs us from having to deal with reality. The reality though, is it becomes tougher and tougher to deal with the separation when you are physically hung over after being wasted.

- The best way to deal with your separation is to find another activity that will allow you to relax and feel renewed so you can deal with the realities associated with your separation – activities such as walking, gardening, listening to music, reading, yoga, meditation, or whatever makes you relax and brings joy.

- Obsessing or Excessive Worry Over Whether the Children Are All Right – I often see this situation occurring with custodial parents. These parents want the best for their children and want to ensure their well-being is not affected by the separation. Usually these parents become so absorbed into their children's lives they have little or no social life outside of their children. They often fear something may happen to their children if they are not there to care for them. This thinking even carries over when the children are with the other parent, and it is not unusual to find out they are complaining about or accusing the other parent of neglecting the children's needs because that parent did not coddle the child. If this behavior becomes excessive, the parent unconsciously takes their anger out on the children for not having any time for themself. If you find yourself doing such behavior allow your children to try challenges on their own without jumping in to do it for them, and when the children return from seeing their other parent listen to what they have done without questioning them, or contact the other parent to scold them. Gradually your insecurity that they are ok will subside and you will feel a sense of relief knowing the children are capable of growing up on their own.

FAMILY MEDIATOR/FAMILY MEDIATION

Family Mediation provides an alternative process to legal means of resolving family issues, dividing assets, and seeking a separation and divorce. Mediation provides a confidential, non-adversarial process through which couples can negotiate part or all of their own settlement with the assistance of a mediator, an impartial third party. In other words, a couple is not pitted against each other, but is assisted by a mediator to work on resolving issues that arise from their disputes, conflicts, differences of opinion, or points of view in a fair and equitable process to reach agreement on their issues. During mediation couples can and do experience intense feelings from emotionally charged issues. However, difficult and challenging issues can be mutually resolved without feeling or believing there is a winner or loser, rather a win-win situation for both and the family.

Mediation, and or, some form of negotiation between couples, with a knowledgeable skilled professional, is the best means to mutually resolve difficult and outstanding issues between couples, especially when reaching agreement on the best interests of the children. Often custody and access matters dealt with through the courts, or between parents without professional assistance results in issues not being satisfactorily resolved, having to be revisited numerous times to the detriment of all involved, especially the children. Such unsettled circumstances can cause children to feel caught up by the separation/divorce and conflicted about loyalties toward each parent.

In order for mediation to proceed and be successful, both parties despite their reasons for entering into this process, must be open to sharing information and be willing to discuss, listen and make adjustments to ideas presented for the best interests of all involved.

Mediation can assist parents to resolve their differences at any stage of their separation, and or, divorce. However, the earlier a couple or parents avail themselves of mediation, the less possibility of the conflict escalating, and the less likelihood of trauma for the children. The guidelines established by a mediator often elevate problems that may occur when parents are reassured they are not going to lose contact with their children.

Mediators can fill a number of different roles based on their experience, background and qualifications. When interviewing to hire a mediator ask about their broad work history not just related to mediation itself, ask about their training, and how they measure success. Some mediators come from counseling backgrounds, from humanistic perspectives, some have knowledge of the legal system, or are lawyers who practice mediation, and others work as Separation/Divorce Coaches who have formal training and backgrounds in family or divorce studies.

The greater a mediator's experience and solid their background the better prepared and able they are to discern what issues are important to each person and assist them in coming to a resolution. They can assist couples sort out matters concerning family heirlooms; encourage clients to separate financial issues from custody and access (visitation) issues; and, help parents to understand their children are not chattel or property. A knowledgeable mediator can also explain the benefits of establishing a parenting plan, which results in a greater likelihood that both parents remain involved, that the children will not be greatly adversely affected by the divorce, and that there will be less chance of future conflict and litigation after an agreement.

There are a number of different styles of mediation to be aware of before settling on any mediator. Lawyers who have training in mediation can conduct mediation and, while working for you their client, will work with the other lawyer/mediator or mediator to resolve the outstanding issues of both parties. A common practice is that both parties agree upon and work with the assistance of an individual mediator to mutually resolve their issues. Another practice is dual gender mediation – one male and one female mediator, who work together with the couple or family. Often this is beneficial to both parties providing gender balance to the process, especially when one party perceives the other to have more power. A team is better able to keep control and facilitate the negotiating process. Another advantage to dual mediators is that you gain two perspectives on an issue and both mediators may find it easier to monitor the process.

Mediators also have many different approaches. Some mediators only handle financial issues; others deal with only custody and access (visitation) issues. Some, as mentioned, work with or in government sponsored agencies; the courts, family service agencies; others, in private practice. Some mediators only see parents or adult couples, some work with entire families. There is even a difference for time spent with clients – some work for a few hours a week, while others work with clients, families through many sessions at a time. Whatever the style/setting for mediation and frequency of sessions make sure you are comfortable with the process itself, as the sessions can be emotionally draining. It is important you leave time between sessions to digest what you have heard and said, and feel recharged enough to continue mediation. Most importantly, you need to feel comfortable and confident that the mediator can assist you and your family to bring about an outcome of positive change in spousal positions and in parental attitudes that will benefit the children.

Here is a sampling of the benefits of Mediation:

a) *Resolution* of issues, all or in part, based upon a mutual agreement.

b) *The* process of reaching an agreement done with the assistance of an impartial third party often ensures the settlement reached is better suited to meeting the couple's and family's needs.

c)   *The* best interests of children can be addressed and mutually resolved.

d)   *Agreements* reached through mediation concerning custody and access will usually only require fine-tuning as, for example children grow older, rather than having to return to court for a hearing to determine or show cause for most changes to be made.

e)   *Mediation* can best incorporate children's feelings and wants through parental discussion, or with direct input from the child themselves. (As a mediator, I would not recommend including a child younger then a developmental age of 12 years to ensure they are capable of understanding and be able to articulate their feeling and thoughts.)

f)   *Despite* mediation requiring greater participation and energy of the party involved, the process is generally cheaper and can be completed in less time than the legal process.

g)   *Mediation* focuses on the future by enabling both parties to implement their mutually agreed plan, which having established an agreement fosters cooperation to resolve future matters when and if they arise.

h)   *At* anytime during the mediation process if the couple, parents, or parties involved reach an impasse, and or, the mediator believes continuing process would not be of benefit to anyone involved, the process could be ended without penalty to the parties involved.

In a number of provinces, such as Manitoba, and states, such as California, mediation is mandatory prior to court. This means there are mandatory entry into mediation programs through which parties must first see a court appointed mediator, a family justice worker, or court mediator to attempt to resolve their family issues outside the court. As with all mediation, the primary purpose of this process is to reduce the conflict between couples and parents to enhance the welfare and well-being of the adults, family and children. As an individual and dual mediator, I accomplish this by supporting and encouraging couples and parents to mutually develop a flexible and manageable strategy, and or, parenting plan. By doing so, couples are able to move forward with their lives. In addition, as parents they are able to define parental roles and provide a safe and nurturing environment for their children, as well as, maintain ongoing close contact with their children after the separation and divorce.

The role for most mediators is as follows:

1.   To give couples, and or, parents the opportunity to discuss their issues, to explore alternatives, and find ways of resolving their differences.

2. To ensure everyone that needs to be involved i.e. children/youth have the opportunity to speak and be heard.

3. The mediator supports and facilitates discussion of both parties issues allowing you to feel "safe" and feel you are being assisted to negotiate a separation/divorce settlement that is fair to both parties (and children)

4. To ensure the setting for mediation is safe, non-adversarial and that participants understand and agree to # 2 above.

5. To assist couples to untie the knot, and assist parents to sort out their spousal roles from parental roles so they can focus on their children's needs and develop frequent and ongoing contact with their children.

6. To encourage dialogue between parents to address their children's needs.

7. To assist parents to concentrate on their present spousal and parental roles instead of dwelling on past conflict.

8. To provide third party insight, information and education to ensure all parties make the best-informed decisions.

9. To support through providing information and encouragement for parents to maintain a cooperative family network that includes all relatives and significant persons i.e. stepparents, step grandparents, grandparents and extended family.

10. To support and encourage each adult, and or, parent and child feel comfortable and safe to voice his or her own opinions.

11. To encourage couples/parents to settle issues amicably and cooperatively that enables adults to make changes over time.

12. To assist parents to develop a parenting plan, consistent with their family and children's needs, and

13. To refer an adult, parent or family member to another professional, and or counselor as needed.

Here are a few examples of common situations seen in mediation:

Tim, the father of two children, was having difficulty being able to express his wishes and concerns about being a parent. His frustration rose as the issue of parenting became more intense. He shut down either because he had trouble expressing his feelings, or he would become angry raising his voice, leaning forward in his seat and clenching his fists by his side. In a role as a counselor, I spoke to Tim away from mediation and asked Tim to explain how he dealt with other difficult situations at work, with friends and with colleagues. Tim described how he resolved matters in a few situations. And even though as he said, "there is more at stake here with his personal situation", I asked him to apply those skills to resolving parenting issues. Once back at mediation, Tim sat back in his chair, listened, and if he wanted to reply or address some matter he would be patient, write it down if need be, and address it when it was his time without interruption. Tim's frustration subsided, his partner Heather felt she was heard, and he felt he was able to convey his wishes too. To the delight of both they were able to mutually address their parenting issues.

Issues concerning the division of assets and financial matters were resolved quickly and amicably. However, Penny was adamant about how parenting was to occur, as she had been the primary care giver before the separation. Her position was there would be no discussion on this subject – it was her way and her way only, as he did little before so shall he now. Both Penny and Frank shared their experiences as a parent. What emerged from the discussion was that Penny felt overwhelmed by the responsibilities of doing much of the parenting. Frank believed he had contributed to the family by providing for their needs. He also felt he did a lot with his children. Discussion, through an educative process, about how each of them communicated to each other followed, and specifically, addressed how each communicated about parenting issues. What emerged was that Penny was not getting Frank's attention on matters she felt needed attending to quickly and felt she had to repeat things repeatedly to get him to participate. Frank felt bombarded the minute he entered the house, badgered by Penny's comments, resulting in him shutting down or protesting by doing activities on his own time. Neither talked about sharing parenting issues. I discussed with them the differences between spousal and parenting responsibilities and ways to set up initial steps to assist them in communicating with each other on parenting matters. This led to the development of a parenting plan helping to reduce family conflict, addressed the parents' and their children's needs, and allowed them to develop a more positive parent-child interaction.

Trudy and Jim amicably resolved issues concerning financial matters and division of assets. They also agreed upon parenting arrangements, however the details of the arrangement seemed quite restrictive and inflexible. In my role as a mediator, I presented them with information on the latest parenting research. After listening and discussing how they could use the information Jim and Trudy formulated a different parenting plan. The information provided to Trudy and Jim revealed parenting practices that would be beneficial to both of them as parents and their children and allowed them to make the best-informed decision regarding their parenting roles.

As a family mediator, I also practice the following:

Any outcome or resolution from mediation is based on a fair and mutual agreement between the couple, parents, and any other party present, i.e. children. Mediation of family issues should be child –centered. In other words, spousal and parenting responsibilities should be addressed separately and emphasis should be placed on finding resolution to issues reflecting a child's needs and from a cooperative parenting perspective, if possible. Parents should be informed of the best parenting practices available in order that they can make the best-informed decisions that may benefit their family. This includes educating and informing parents of the consequences of the loss of parent –child relationships, and or, interaction, and the benefit of positive parental communication and cooperation. Finally, the language of the mediation agreement is written in clear, concise words and phrases that reflect how both you and your ex feel and believe is the spirit of what you have discussed and agreed upon.

Couples, and or, parents can begin mediation at any time – they can do so to settle a separation and divorce; enter into mediation while pursuing another course of action i.e. legal proceedings; or, start mediation after a separation/divorce agreement to resolve outstanding issues not resolved or covered by the initial agreement.

How long the mediation process will take, will of course depend on your circumstances. However, the general process a mediator follows is: First, they will interview each party to mediation separately (including children if they will be part of the mediation). Next, the mediator will review and determine areas of common ground and areas that need further discussion from the information gathered. The mediator will then arrange a time for the parties to come together to discuss this information and set an agenda of their wants and needs with respect to the issues they present. Each issue is reviewed, discussed, and summarized. Finally, ideas, ways and means to implement resolution to some or all of the issues raised are drafted into a written agreement, and reviewed again by the parties (and often is reviewed with a lawyer) before the agreement is signed.

In the case of child-custody agreements, to ensure it is an enforceable and binding legal document, it must be written up, signed by both parents and by a family judge or commissioner, and filed by the court. It is then a court order, and if a problem arises, either party may file an application or notice of motion to change the court order, and or, return to mediation.

In your agreement set up with individual or dual mediators there should be a clause outlining that at anytime during the process any party, including the mediator, can end the process. Generally, a mediator before this occurs will discuss the situation, known as an impasse, with one or both parties to ensure nothing is overlooked before mediation ends. In some cases, the process may end, but resume once new information, or the situation that caused the impasse changes. Situations that cause mediation to end are:

If a mediator finds them self caught by family circumstances unaware of the family dynamics, becomes overwhelmed by the process, and or, loses objectivity; if one party continues despite efforts by the mediator to refrain from name calling etc.;

Final Word for couples and parents: It takes courage and selflessness to examine your relationship from a holistic perspective, rather from your own point of view. Keeping with this perspective enables couples to be more open and receptive to resolving issues raised during mediation. And, it takes great courage for parents to recognize their own attitudes and behaviors detrimental to their children, such as switching their thinking of children as "mine" to thinking of children are "ours". Such a perspective allows parents to focus on resolving issues from the best interests of their children.

FAMILY LAW LAWYER/NOTARY

A Notary is a person who has legal authority to swear documents, exhibits and affidavits, which can then filed with your court documents for your separation and divorce. Using a notary will save you money; however, you will not receive any legal advice interpreting the information contained in your documents. However, direction may be given with respect to the set up of a document to ensure it can be filed according to court/administrative standards and processed. In the case of couples that seek to obtain a divorce by means of the do-it-yourself-divorce kit, using a notary is certainly the option to keep costs at a minimum. However, if you have any questions or concerns regarding filling out the court documents, and or, information that is required to complete these forms you will need to see a family law lawyer.

The most influential person on your team may be your family law lawyer, if you choose the legal process to resolve your partnership, and or, matrimonial matter. As mentioned, some family law lawyers have training and experience in family mediation. Decide on what course of action you wish to pursue.

(When selecting a lawyer see N.B. section located at the beginning of this chapter to assist you with your selection.) If you do not have referrals, or feel you need other choices other than the referrals you have, one place to begin is to locate a lawyer by contacting your provincial law society or state bar and ask if they have an accreditation system for family lawyers. Then you can choose two or three in your area for interviews.

Some people choose a lawyer solely based on their reputation, basing their decision that the lawyer's impact will WOW the other lawyer and influence the other spouse. A word of caution, though this may get you the desired effect, it has been my experience such a strategy often backfires and is only short term. People spend big bucks to hire a 'top gun' to over power their spouse instead of spending money on other things, especially on their children, and the result usually is the other party feels 'wronged' and will repeatedly return to court to mitigate circumstances. Most importantly, children will suffer not just from the economic loss, but also emotionally as they wrestle with their loyalties to support both parents.

Reasons to consult a Lawyer:

- ▶ You decide to proceed by legal means rather than an alternative
- ▶ Your partner/spouse has told you they have consulted a lawyer
- ▶ Your partner/spouse has been violent with you and/or the children
- ▶ Your partner/spouse does not provide support for your children
- ▶ Your partner/spouse has left you without talking about plans first
- ▶ You do not know your legal rights
- ▶ You do not know how the divorce laws affect your particular situation
- ▶ Your partner/spouse has threatened to take or has taken the children

If any of these statements apply to you, it would be wise to seek the advice of a family law lawyer, if you have not done so already. Seeing a family law expert does not mean you need to decide to obtain a legal separation or divorce. Your first step is to seek their advice and obtain information.

Here are a few pointers to remember when hiring a lawyer:

1. Is the lawyer you choose a family law specialist? How long have they been practicing? Have they had cases like yours and how did they deal with them? If you are reviewing a mediation agreement, you should also hire a family law specialist. Refer to the note at the beginning of this chapter.

2. You should choose a lawyer who can think outside the box. In other words, choose a person who is flexible and creative in finding alternatives to resolving your issues. i.e. providing mediation instead going to court, or finding a

divorce coach to manage stress/grief instead of escalating the acrimony between the spouses by filing more motions in court.

3. Do not choose a lawyer who will pass you off to a junior lawyer. If you hire a lawyer, unless you have agreed to others working on your case you should expect conversations, meetings, court appearances handled by the person you hired.

4. DO NOT USE the same lawyer your spouse has, or who is associated with your spouse's family in any way. If your separation/divorce becomes bitter, you want a lawyer whose alliances lie with you.

5. Resist the urge to use the same lawyer as your spouse, even if your agreement appears simple, sound, or if it seems cost effective to do so. You, as well as your partner/spouse, require objective advice.

6. DO NOT USE your lawyer as an emotional outlet. Pouring your emotions out on your lawyer with cost you time and ultimately money. If you are having difficulty coming to terms with the loss of your partnership/marriage it would be best to see a grief coach, counselor, and or divorce coach to help you deal with these issues. Keep your relationship with your lawyer on a strictly business level by allowing your lawyer to assist you the best he or she can by dealing with the legal aspects.

7. When interviewing a lawyer, or seeing a lawyer for a consultation prior to possibly hiring them, do the following: Prepare and ask questions that apply to your situation, not general family law questions, as your time and theirs is valuable. Come prepared with a brief but detailed overview or summary of your story (see below for further details). Ask the lawyer, given these facts, how and what can be done legally. If you do not understand or require further explanation, ask. Don't relinquish control of this matter that can effect and have tremendous impact on your future to someone without understanding and knowing the process – after all, you wouldn't have someone paint your house by them telling you don't worry I'll take care of all the details. You owe it to yourself, to ensure your well being, that you understand what your lawyer is going to do for you.

After you have visited a lawyer, ask yourself the following questions: (Having reviewed the divorce laws for your state or province better prepares you in answering the following questions.) How confident are you they were listening and heard your wishes and needs? Do you feel or think they will work with you? How comfortable are you in their abilities? If they obtain a divorce settlement for you can you be satisfied with the outcome? How you answer these questions, will determine whether you will hire that lawyer or find someone else to obtain your separation/divorce.

Prior to seeing a lawyer prepare, as mentioned, an overview of your relationship and family life, beginning with the courtship phase. Be brief, give enough detail it outlines the highlights and lows, but not so detailed as to become a novel like War of the Roses. You should include a brief description and length of the courtship phase; when you began living together; details of the conditions of how you lived (i.e. was it a volatile relationship? If so, how? Were there difficulties? When, how often and for what reasons? Etc.); details of any counseling that you or the other person took; your financial history – who supported whom? What did you do before you were married? Moreover, did you work while in the relationship, or while married? If you stopped work what was the reason?; If you have children, when were each of the children born?; Were there any significant changes in your relationship/partnership after each child's birth?; How do both of you parent? Has your parenting styles contributed to the decision to end your relationship?; What are the current living arrangements?; What are your thoughts and feelings about what you would consider to be acceptable and unacceptable circumstances regarding custody and access – what do you want for you children and yourself after separation and divorce?; and, what events/circumstances (reasons) have moved you to decide upon obtaining a separation/divorce? Also, ask questions about and share your wishes regarding division of common assets and shared/joint business matters. If during the discussion of these issues with a lawyer you feel yourself being wound up, refer back to your notes.

This should allow you to refocus on the issues. Venting your anger is fine, however doing so may potentially sidetrack you from telling your complete story and may cost you more money in doing so.

Come prepared with the following information in a written form:

- Your full legal name and any a.k.a. names; your address (work and home), your telephone number, and other means of contact (cellular, fax, e-mail, etc.), and include all addresses you have lived at in the past two years;

- Your date and place of birth, date and place of marriage, and date of separation;

- If you are not a citizen by birth, you should include the date you came to the country and the length of residence by province or state;

- A copy of the marriage certificate. If not, and married elsewhere, information on how it can be obtained i.e. government agency and its address/phone number;

- The details of all previous marriages, including the surname of your ex-spouse, and a copy of the decree absolute if it's available;

- Your spouse's full legal name and any a.k.a. names; his address (work and home), his telephone number, and other means of contact (cellular, fax, e-mail, etc.), date and country of birth, and the name of your spouse's lawyer, if you know it;

- If you have children, include their names, their dates of birth, and the schools and grades they attend; and,

- Financial details for both of you (family and business assets); level of education; employment history; net worth prior to marriage, net worth at separation and contributions made to your family.

- An inventory (deeds plus bank statements concerning mortgage payments) of your property and other assets i.e. boat, cottage etc.

Finally, if after your consultation with a lawyer, and after you have considered the pointers stated previously, you decide to hire the lawyer you have spoken with, be prepared to discuss and pay a retainer. Find out what their hourly office rate is and what their rate is to attend court – these are usually different. Inquire as to whether, they will use a law clerk or junior lawyer to do research and preparatory work on your case. If they do, ask how the clerk's or junior lawyer's time is billed. And, be aware that every telephone call, every message left, every piece of investigative work, every letter will usually cost you money – so ask if this is the case, so there are no surprises when you receive an invoice, or asked for a further retainer. If you have any questions about billing ask. Make sure you are comfortable with the method of payment and billing practices before you provide a retainer.

I worked with clients (I will call them) Ted and Sherri who paid a retainer but did not enquire as to what activities could be expensed out from their retainer. Each was surprised and dumb founded to see they were charged for time they had spent with their lawyer on the telephone. Sherri said, "I'd call [my lawyer's office] to ask how things were going and either spoke to my lawyer or [their] assistant and was charged for the call.

I thought I wouldn't be charged for finding out what was going on with my case."

It is understandable to feel you may have been over charged, however it is your responsibility to ask about billing practices. Ted, as well, was billed for work his lawyer had stated was part of his practice. "The lawyer", Ted said, "spoke to my spouse's lawyer outside the courtroom to reach a settlement. I was surprised when I'd receive a bill for this work." Unfortunately, Ted did not question the lawyer as to how providing this service would be billed. You need to understand your lawyer's billing practices so this does not happen to you.

Insist upon regular billings, preferably on a monthly basis to ensure you have a solid understanding of the activities going on with your case. In addition, if you are thinking you are going to receive a lump settlement, and wanting to pay your lawyer from this, make sure you discuss this with your lawyer and make a plan for repayment that works for both of you. Also, find out the rate, when a service charge will be added to the bill for outstanding balances.

A lawyer should be able to explain the range of possible outcomes for your case based on their experience. They should be able to explain the strong and weak points of your case, that worst scenario you can anticipate, an approximate period to reach a settlement in or out of court, as well as a reasonable cost for services. If a lawyer guarantees you results, seek out a second opinion.

Some lawyers represent their client's best interest by working by any means to resolve the outstanding relationship, matrimonial and family issues.

Dana and Al, parents of a young boy, were stuck arguing about parenting issues outside the courtroom and each was threatening to return to court to get their position heard and upheld in court. Both lawyers recognizing this was not in the best interests of their clients negotiated a temporary plan for access based on a consensus of their ideas. As part of the temporary agreement, I was called by one of the lawyers, on behalf of both parties, to draft a graduated parenting plan addressing the concerns of both parents. Both parents accepted the plan as a good initial agreement and their lawyers asked that it be included as part of the court order that would be reviewed in three months. The work each of their lawyers did caused not only a legal settlement to be reached, but set the ground work for both parents to participate in mediation to resolve communication issues that were the root of their escalating bantering in court.

While some other lawyers will represent their client by upholding their client's wishes and work within legal means to resolve relationship, matrimonial and family issues from their client's perspective. Rick, a father of a four-year-old boy, believed because of ex's anger towards him she was denying him access to see their son. The lawyer reinstated access by means of a court order to be supervised over the course of three months in order that the supervisor could observe and verify that Rick was capable of parenting his son, and that the rapport between he and his son was positive. The lawyer returned to court with a positive report from the supervisor and a court order was drafted not only allowing unsupervised access, but also set out a regular schedule for Rick to visit his son.

Others will advise their clients as to areas that they believe may be unrealistic wishes or goals and counsel them on what they believe would be a more realistic approach to obtaining a settlement. Lawyers for both parents were representing their client's, each of who was asking for custody of their three-year-old daughter.

Sandra had been the primary care giver during the first year and a half of their daughter's life, due to her spouse's mental health. However, Kevin had been responsible for parenting during the last sixteen months up to the time of the court hearing, as Sandra was in and out of rehab dealing with her alcohol dependency. A family conference was held with the parents, lawyers and the judge. From the information Sandra disclosed: that she had just received her two-month sobriety pin; that she had just started a new job and recently found an apartment, her lawyer advised, even though all this was positive and she had shown she had been a positive parent it would be best for their daughter that Kevin have temporary custody. The lawyer advised Sandra it would be too soon for her to take on care giving responsibilities when she just stabilized her own life. The lawyer further encouraged Sandra to continue the positive work on herself because this will enable her to be a positive influence in her daughter's life. Sandra initially did not enthusiastically take to this counsel; however, after mauling over it over agreed this would be best for both herself and her daughter. The lawyers arranged a consent order that Kevin have temporary physical custody of their daughter, and because Sandra was capable of parenting and had a positive rapport with her daughter, generous and liberal access was ordered with the order to be revisited in six months. Six months later, both parents were granted joint custody and a schedule was drafted that enabled their daughter to live part of the week with each parent.

If you are unsure, which process is best for you, then get a second opinion to ensure you gain a clear and thorough perspective. It is important to measure the likelihood of achieving your wants and goals for yourself against the toll on your emotional and financial well-being, and that of your family's well being. It is up to you to decide the issues you contest are worth the expense and effort, and which issues will not be dealt with legally. Deal with important issues that have to do with parenting and children, as decisions made about these matters have long-term consequences into the future.

A final comment: All too often, I am aware of individuals and couples who seem to hand over authority and guidance regarding their relationship, matrimonial and family issues to the lawyer they've hired carte blanch, then step back and await the result only to be dumb founded and devastated by the outcome. It cannot be over emphasized, underscored, and mentioned enough that you need to question, ask and give direction to the lawyer you hire.

DIVORCE COACH

In the broadest sense of the term, anyone who works with adults, children and families to assist them in resolving issues concerned with their separation and divorce acts as a divorce coach. The profession of Divorce Coach itself is relatively new (the last ten years or so), and the role and duties of a Coach vary widely, just as in other professions, so check to see if their qualifications and experience fit the services they offer. Almost all divorce coaches will have an undergraduate degree in Psychology, Social Work or Child/Family Studies and, equally important, and should have a great deal of working experience and knowledge with separated and divorced children and families. In addition, most coaches will have higher levels of education, Master and Doctorate degrees, specializing in studies focusing on family and divorce. Likewise, their working experience and knowledge has been focused and concentrated on separated and divorced children and families.

As mentioned, the role and duties of a Divorce Coach can vary. The following is a list and explanation of services offered as part of my practice. Other coaches may provide some, all or similar services to these:

1. Separation and Divorce Coaching – First, a coach will meet, and or, speak to the individual, couple or family that has contacted him/her to find out and identify what course of action would be best suited to address the issues raised by their particular situation.

In the case of Penny and Frank who we discussed previously, they resolved their divorce and parenting issues by means of mediation. Prior to this process however, I was initially contacted and spoke with Frank. After listening to the issues he brought up, we talked about the one issue he believed would be the most difficult to resolve – being involved in the parenting of his children. "I want to be able to be apart of their lives", he said, "not just doing activities with them, but being a parent to them." He was asked to describe what he thought this might look like, what was the past and current parenting situation, and what he believed was preventing him from being able to parent. What emerged from the discussion with Frank was that he had sporadically been involved in the parenting of their children during the past, and despite being willing and available to parent for the past year or so, he was parenting on a limited basis. Frank revealed that Penny having gone through inconsistent parenting by Frank did not want to relinquish parenting out of fear his behavior would relapse to what it had in the past. Further discussion led to him allowing me to contact Penny to speak with her about their pending divorce and parenting issues. I brought up options to settling matters concerning their divorce. We discussed the option of mediation and she felt this would be a good option. Mediation allowed them the opportunity and means of coming to agreement on all their financial and divorce issues. It also was the best forum to allow Penny to be able to voice her concerns and Frank answers on the issue of parenting. They were then successful in setting up a graduated parenting plan.

As a coach, I have assisted individuals, parents and couples to:

▶ (As with the example above) Learn about options and means

to best resolve and manage separation and divorce issues specific to their situation

▶ Gain an understanding of the communication styles used and learn communication techniques that will reduce tension by expressing their needs in words and actions.

▶ Learn about ideas and steps in the process of creating strategies that will allow them to alleviate conflict and manage stress concerning parenting, custody and access (visitation) and financial/property issues.

▶ Educate and inform couples and parents of similarities and differences between dissolving a living-together relationship and a married relationship

▶ Gain awareness and understanding for them to be able create tools to alleviate stress handling contentious issues

▶ Learn about child-centered parenting strategies for parents to parent, and for children not to be caught in the middle.

▶ *(And for children/youth to)* Recognize their feelings, understand and develop ways of coping with the loss of having a changed family and transitioning between two households

▶ Gain insight and support into managing their feelings around the death of the relationship; loss of being able to parent; (for youth) loss of having a parent being present; loss of family; and, the loss of future expectations, and

▶ Develop strategies to manage their immediate and long-term personal goals

2. Post Separation and Divorce Coaching – Often former partners, former spouses, and or parents call or e-mail about updating parts of their mediation agreement or their existing family plan. They want support, options, and or, strategies to be able to fine-tune these arrangements to reflect and meet current needs.

Mary, with agreement from John, contacted me about updating their existing agreement/court order. They had two twin boys who were now starting middle school and both boys' extra-curriculum activities were taking up a lot of time and were occurring on days when John was to see them. John had also recently moved out of town, commuting into town for work on the days he was scheduled to see the boys. From our conversation, she conveyed her anxiousness to find a solution. We discussed a number of options she could review with John and I mentioned John was welcome to talk to me about any of the ideas we discussed. John phoned to clarify a few points. In this case, as John lived some distance away from the office I encouraged him they could resolve the matter between themselves without having to come to the office. He agreed and so did Mary. To meet the current circumstances John agreed to continue seeing the boys on the existing access days and participate in taking the boys to and from their practices. This enabled Mary not to have to do this task freeing her time up to do other things. His access time increased to allow him and the boys to have dinner on those days. Overnight visits were changed to flexible weekend sleepovers depending on the boy's activities. In addition, John would travel into town to take them to their activities on weekends when he did not have them for sleepovers.

3. Family Mediation – As a family mediator, I act as a neutral third party facilitator for both parties, and or, their children if included, to assist in creating in whole or part a mutually agreed upon plan/agreement that addresses their needs. (See section on Mediation)

4. Grief Coaching – Too often adults and children have difficulty managing and being able to cope with feelings regarding the loss of their relationship; loss of expectations of what the future would be like in their family; loss of their former family structure; and, loss of not being with, and or, interacting with their parents the way they previously have. Providing support and insight into the emotional process (See section on the emotional process of divorce for details) that children and adults experience during separation and divorce enables them to learn about tools, techniques and strategies they can develop and use to manage their grief caused by one or a few of these areas.

5. Access Supervision (Visitation) – The role of an access supervisor is to provide unbiased, third party observations on the interaction and rapport between parent and child, guardian and child, and or, adult and child. The primary purpose of providing supervision is to ensure the safety and well-being of the children involved. Along with its primary purpose, supervised access is also a means by which a child can have their voice heard about wanting to see and be with their other parent. The supervisor is not out of eye and ear contact while observing access, and may discreetly take notes during access time or immediately following, to be able to prepare written reports, and or, provide testimony in court, if necessary. Such a specialized service and should be provided by professionals with clinical experience observing children and families. In other words, such professionals should have both training and experience observing children and families in some of the areas such as social service facilities – treatment and assessment centers, and in community settings – community centers, schools and family homes. In some regions in Canada and in some parts of the United States, supervisors also adhere to policies and guidelines outlined by the Supervised Access Network, an organization established to develop and maintain standards for those who provide access supervision.

Such training and experience is necessary as supervised access is perhaps the most undervalued and most misused tool available to parents and social service professionals. Often it is asked, even demanded by one parent, and accepted by, and or, court enforced upon the non-custodial parent for varied reasons. Some of the main reasons for access supervision include: long absence of a parent seeing their child; concerns of parent behaving inappropriately; lack of parent skills; concern the parent may manipulate, coerce, and or, bad-mouth the custodial parent in child's presence; concern of child abduction; access parent may be abusive toward child; a custodial parent uses this process to retaliate against the other parent; and, having a supervisor involved to observe can verify and corroborate parenting abilities of the access parent, eliminating the need for supervision. From a professional supervisor's perspective, access supervision (supervised visitation) is one of, if not the only time when a child's observed behavior speaks loudly about their want and desire regarding their non-custodial parent. It is a vital means to maintaining a sense of rapport and connectedness for both parent and child, both during and after separation/divorce.

OTHER SOCIAL SERVICE PROFESSIONALS

Family support workers, social workers, counselors, and psychologists in your community who work with families and children can and are often are a good resource for finding and locating information and services you will require. Some social workers, counselors, and psychologists, whose practice deals specifically with families, may be able to provide insight concerning aspects of the family dynamics you possibly may encounter. They may also specialize in offering grief counseling to be able to manage the loss of the relationship, expectations, etc. often experienced due to the break up of a relationship/marriage.

FINANCIAL ADVISOR/PLANNER

A financial advisor is an individual who understands the principles of family law as it pertains to regulating the financial aspects of divorce.

They should be a PFP, Professional Financial Planner standing or equivalent to provide such advice. A financial planner is not necessarily an expert on every financial detail with regard to divorce, but rather has the ability to pull all the financial details together into a coherent financial plan.

A financial advisor/planner should be able to offer services in three areas for individuals/couples considering or experiencing a divorce:

DIVORCE PLANNING:

- Financial entitlements (e.g. capital assets marriage vs. common-law)
- Assets (e.g. pensions, registered savings plan, work benefits, frequent flyer miles, etc.)
- Liability planning (how to restructure, re-finance, and or, repay debt)

FINANCIAL PLANNING:

- Division of assets and liabilities
- Transfers between capital and income
- Tax implications and forecasts
- Financial planning before, during and after divorce (budget and financial planning to meet financial goals)

INVESTMENT PLANNING:

- Converting investments into income or vice versa
- Budget planning to reach retirement goal
- Establishing financial objectives and options during and after divorce
- Developing a detailed investment plan

**REALTOR

Most home sellers rely on the expertise of hiring a licensed realtor to represent them in the sale of their home or property. The realtor prices the property with the assistance of various resources available to them from previous sales in the general neighborhood – MLS data, trends, and the general condition of the property and improvements. A *list contract* is entered into between the real estate firm and the seller. The *listing contract* will specify the date the agreement is entered into, the fee or commission to be paid, the parties on the contract, the expiry date, and any other terms agreed to between the parties.

The realtor through their real estate company (the agent) is to perform the duties that will encourage a *Contract of Purchase and Sale* to be offered to the sellers of the property. Upon the acceptance by the all the parties to the *Contract of Purchase and Sale,* and subsequent removal of any 'conditions' such as financing, building inspection, etc. the property will therein be transferred to the new owner(s), usually through the services of a law firm or notary.

Particular to the Divorce, Separation, or Estate Settlement situations there are circumstances whereby the parties cannot agree on a realtor, or wish to be represented separately. In this instance, two realtors can be hired to 'co-list' the property, with each of them having a 'fiduciary duty' to each of the parties, meaning a duty to act, in this case, for both sellers' benefit not their own. This gives the parties a second level of protection, and removes doubt one party will gain an advantage over the other.

**REAL ESTATE APPRAISER

In many cases, the parties obtain two bona fide professionally trained appraisals from certified appraisers from different firms. Sometimes the courts will order this, or it is done by mutual agreement between the parties. This can further diffuse an awkward or difficult situation, particularly if one party is more knowledgeable than the other concerning the real estate market. The lenders (banks, credit unions, etc.) will not advance monies on conventional mortgages either without a professional appraisal, or at the very least, a copy of the provincial or state assessment record to prove the minimum value. Therefore, the appraisal carries considerable power, and is a document the banks, credit unions, etc, rely heavily on to lend money towards sale, and thus purchase of a property. Appraisals more than 90 days old would need to be updated for lending purposes, or to establish present value for the parties.

**CONVEYANCE

This is the term used when the services of a lawyer are required to transfer the title of the property. The necessary documentation to transfer the title of the property, discharge any mortgages, liens, or other encumbrances on the title are done by them. The lawyer will handle the monies from the transaction through their *Trust Account,* and there is an *undertaking* by the lawyer to convey those funds from one party to the other through a second lawyer. Many times, one or more of the parties to the transaction may be buying again, and the lawyer for that party would normally handle the new transaction as well. In cases of Divorce, Separation, and estate settlements there is usually more than one lawyer involved. Each party has the right to their own representation, and it is advised, that they seek independent legal advice in all matters related to the conveyance of real estate property.

** FOR SPECIFIC INFORMATION ABOUT REALTORS, APPRAISERS AND CONVEYANCE CONTACT YOUR LOCAL REAL ESTATE FIRM TO FIND OUT THE SPECIFIC RULES IN YOUR AREA.

Just as in the construction of a house, you have now laid the foundation and set down the framework – 'the bones', as referred to in the housing industry, upon which you can now prepare and create the features you want. The healthier 'the bones' the fewer problems will arise as the house ages, and so too, the stronger your foundation and development of a plan the healthier your possible outcome will be to obtain a separation or divorce. The remainder of the book discusses how you want the house – your separation/divorce to look and feel like depending on what is attached to the frame, walls and roof of the house. Discussed are issues concerning the children, custody, access, communication and special circumstances.

Chapter Three

What About The Children?

▶ Events and Behaviors by Parents Can Have a Tremendous Affect on Children

▶ Comments and Illustrations tell parents what children feel and think about their parents' divorce

▶ Strengthening your Relationship with Your Children

Parenting is a challenge in the very best of times, and one of the most difficult challenges occurs when a child's parents separate and divorce. The task of 'Ex's is to remain parenting partners and to provide, nurture and create a sense of well-being for their children – of feeling loved, cared for and having a sense of security. This is of prime importance, as research indicates that children whose parents demonstrate committed and cooperative attitudes during and following divorce, such that their children are able to continue enjoying active relationships with both their mother and father, are those children that adjust best. A crucial example of this occurs when parents announce the separation, and or, divorce to their children.

THE 'ANNOUNCEMENT' OF THE DECISION TO SEPARATE/DIVORCE TO YOUR CHILDREN

The first significant challenge for parents, who no longer see themselves as couple, is how they can best inform the children of their decision to separate, and or, divorce. When children perceive their family life to be disintegrating, they suffer a sense of security (a loss of feeling wanted) and a sense of well-being. If you and your ex are able to work together and agree upon how and what shall be announced and you minimize the shock and loss of their feeling adrift without a life raft. In order to do this you don't have to like each other, except respect them as a parent and focus on what is important – your child's well-being.

There are several positive reasons to tell your children about your decision to separate or divorce: First, by announcing and explaining your decision to divorce together, you are showing your children, that despite the difference between you as a couple, you are unified in making decisions together as parents. Doing so demonstrates to the children they still have parents who love and care for them, despite the 'shock' of the situation.

It demonstrates to them 'a new kind of family'. Second, your children may have been experiencing anxiety prior to the 'announcement' simply because of the uncertainty they have felt with the family environment. Telling them of your decision to divorce will eliminate much of this anxiety, despite an announcement they most likely do not want to hear. Third, don't your children deserve to be told by their parents who love them, rather than finding out about it 'outside the family'? Hearing such a decision from you, and better still if possible, from the both of you, allows you to be there to reassure your children that you love them, and allows them the opportunity to ask and have any questions they may have answered. Finally, if no reconciliation is possible and the decision to divorce is definite, the sooner an announcement is made to your children the less general anxiety they may experience and the sooner they can begin to resolve their own grief process, necessary for them to adjust and accept the new look of their family.

Children are very sensitive to the feelings their parents transmit, especially how each parent regards the other. They sense that their enjoyment of both parents depends on how on how both of you are feeling about one another. Children quickly become attune and receptive to non-verbal cues, mannerisms, body language and verbal messages, including tone, that indicates the dynamic between their parents. It is remarkable how much children actually perceive their parents are trying to hide for sakes.

Barbara and Dick's relationship had been distant and very cool for nearly a year before they separated, and both were now in the midst of obtaining a divorce. They had decided it would be best not to disrupt the children by having Dick leave the home and find a place near his work. The next day after the decision had been made and Dick moved his personal belongings Barbara talked to the children, their eight-year-old son and six-year-old daughter. It was clear from their fidgeting, crying by both and then anger, displayed by their son throwing stuff, that the children were overwhelmed by the thought. (Dick spoke to the children prior to taking the children out on their first time together with him.) What was clear to both from the children's comments was that they were insecure not just about having a relationship with their father, but where and how were they going to fit into this 'new family'. Both children had sensed 'things were not right' with their parents for quite awhile. The parents felt the children were feeling lost. After seven weeks had passed since Barbara announced their impending divorce to their children, both Dick and Barbara were advised to work out an arrangement between each other on reintroducing their plan to divorce to the children in a unified way. They were to decide who would say what and how with each other, both comment and reaffirm to the children that both love them, and tell their children the decision to divorce was not their fault by explaining it in simple non-judgmental terms. Also, briefly comment on how the children would see their father (at least in the short term). Dick and Barbara both indicated after their talk with their children that both were less anxious and seemed a lot more like themselves again. Each expressed the wish that seven weeks ago they had done this 'announcement' together.

The partnership for Paul with June had been up and down for many months and there were now far too many downs than ups. Their relationship, despite going to counseling was now at an end. Their separation was anything but amicable, except they could both agree they had a wonderful four-year-old daughter. When approached by the couple concerned with their daughter's sense of well-being, they were told that they each believed and felt the other was a positive parent for their daughter Katie. They were told they had to adjust their attitudes towards one another and see each other as parenting partners. This doesn't require that you have to like each other, just be respectful, friendly and stay focused on matters concerning their daughter. All right, they said, but how? First, keep the language verbally or in writing uncomplicated and focused on matters concerning the care of their daughter. And, when interaction becomes difficult tell yourself this is for your daughter's sake (and yours), or mentally focus and hold a picture of your daughter in your mind while telling yourself this is for your daughter's well-being (and yours too). Their daughter is now seven and Paul and June continue to be parenting partners.

In some families children become aware you are having partner or marital difficulties and ask you about whether you will be splitting up or getting a divorce. This is often an awkward question if you have not made a decision, and or, discussed this with your partner or spouse. The best response is to give an honest non-judgmental reply, perhaps something like this: "Mom/Dad and I are working on some areas we don't agree on. Mom/Dad and I want you to know we both love you very much. I know this is tough for you, and it's been tough for us too, and we will let you know when we reach a decision on these things." Once you make a decision it is best, as indicated above, to make the 'announcement', and ideally, for you to tell the children with your partner or spouse.

Here are certain guidelines you should follow together:

> ▶ *Consider timing* of the 'announcement': DO NOT discuss the decision prior to a child's bedtime; before they are going to school; before they are leaving to go do an outing or activity; or, before they leave to sleep at a friend's house or leave for camp.

DO IT during a quiet time when there is little distraction and turn off phones, TV and radios etc.

▶ It is best for the children, if possible, to provide a unified decision together for the reasons previously mentioned. This is an announcement made by you the parents as to why you are getting a divorce – it is not a subject open for discussion, though at the end you may ask and encourage the children to ask questions.

▶ BRIEFLY state in simple, non-judgmental age appropriate language your reason for the separation/divorce. (You only have 30-45 seconds to get your message across.) Decide how you and your partner will tell the children by writing a brief and simple summary of how you have agreed to tell your children – who and how it is to be said so that neither of you creates conflict or friction for the other. Do not discuss specifics, such as, "Your Mom/Dad met someone else... or, because I'm/they are not good enough for them/me we are getting divorce." Remember the 'blunt' truth may paint one of you as a 'bad' person, which will put the children in an awkward position and may undermine them personally since they are half his/hers.

▶ Stress the fact YOU BOTH STILL LOVE and CARE FOR THEM. *This is important*, as children can and do feel they are some how to blame for your divorce, and or, fear that you may stop loving them if you have stopped loving the other parent. Knowing you love and care for them will elevate much of these negative feeling and thoughts.

▶ Emphasize to your children they were in no way responsible for the decision to divorce and that it is a decision made solely between you and the other parent. Saying this will help eliminate any idea by your children to think they can influence or prevent this decision from occurring.

▶ If possible, briefly outline what custody and access (visitation) arrangements will be, at least in the short term (up to 3 months). Such information provides children with some sense of stability, continuity, and when enforced, allows children a sense of consistency and security.

▶ Making a decision and announcing it to your children allows them to accept the finality of the situation, enabling them to begin the grieving process concerning the present family dynamic and begin to accept a two parent home dynamic for example.

▶ After ending the meeting with your children, make sure that you establish times you can meet with the other parent to firm up plans. It most likely will take more than one meeting, so do not leave each meeting without setting up another meeting date, even if it is cancelled because you have agreed upon arrangements for the time being.

In some situations, it may not be possible for both of you to make the 'announcement' to separate or divorce together and you must tell them by yourself. If this is the case, here are some guidelines for you to follow:

▶ *Consider timing* of the 'announcement': DO NOT discuss the decision prior to a child's bedtime; before they are going to school; before they are leaving to go do an outing or activity; or, before they leave to sleep at a friend's house or leave for camp. DO IT during a quiet time when there is little distraction and turn off phones, TV and radios etc.

▶ Try to select a time when you are feeling calm and feeling able to answer any questions your children may present to you. Allow them to feel they are able express their feelings.

▶ Write down a brief and simple summary of what and how you will tell your children about your reason for getting a divorce. Use non-judgmental age appropriate language your reason for the separation/divorce.

▶ *Speak only for yourself.* Commenting about your partner or spouse can be problematic, in that you may misrepresent them and in doing so will likely cause confusion for your children if they ask questions about it later.

▶ *Don't belittle, degrade or blame your partner or spouse.* Doing so will only cost you respect and put your children in an uncomfortable position. Remember your child's makeup, whether you like it or not, stems from the other parent. So by putting down the other parent, you are actually making the child feel uncomfortable by indirectly putting them down too.

▶ If a partner or spouse has disappeared and disappointed both you and the children, and they are angry about his actions, it is best you acknowledge their anger. Acknowledge the anger by using "I" messages. For example, "I know you are angry that your mother/father left, it's hard for me to accept and I am angry too. However, I want you to know her/his leaving had nothing to do with you or anything you did. I am here, I love you and I want you here with me."

▶ If you know your partner or spouse loves and cares for the children explain this to them. Misrepresenting them will likely cause confusion and anger towards you when your children find out and ask questions about it later.

▶ There are circumstances when are partner or spouse is not able to have or maintain a healthy relationship with their children due to their disappearance, drug, and or alcohol dependence, emotional and mental health issues. It is best to deal with your children's feelings and understanding of the situation as honestly as possible. Don't paint a glowing picture or glorify your spouse/partner to protect your children from the truth, as once the truth is known they will not trust your insincerity.

A point that cannot be over emphasized is adjusting your explanation of the divorce to each child's level of understanding.

CHILDREN OF PRE-SCHOOL AGE:

Children under age five think in concrete terms and will not understand long involved explanations. For example, if you are planning a divorce not a trial living apart/separation use the word 'divorce' and provide a simple illustration of what this means. For instance, "Your Mom/Dad and I are getting a divorce. What this means is that you (and add siblings names) will be living with Mom/Dad here at the house/apartment and Mom/Dad/I will be living nearby/in town in an apartment/house. Tomorrow/Monday (be specific and name the day) your Mom/Dad will take you over to see where they are living." Once you and spouse or partner have discussed at least temporary access or visitation for the children it is best for a child *up to age ten* to have and keep a few personal items, and or toys at the other parent's residence to provide some familiarity and comfort to ease the adjustment of going from one place to another. If this has been done there may be an opportunity at the end of the comment made above to add: "Mom/Dad and I have discussed that it is ok for you to bring over a couple of toys you can keep there so you can play with them there when you see Mom/Dad, if that's ok with you." Keep in mind the tone of voice you use to speak to children of this age, as they will be very sensitive to how you speak to them. Maintaining a soft and calm tone of voice will help reassure your children that you care for them.

CHILDREN OF PRIMARY SCHOOL AGE:

Children, ages five through eight, still think in concrete terms, but want information from the perspective of how it affects them. You should emphasize ways in which their daily routines will stay the same and emphasize the fact your divorce is not their fault. For example, "You are still going to the same school and have the same teacher. You will still be going to cubs or brownies (after school activities, and if you know who is going to take them or pick them up include this in the comment). It is important for you to know our divorce is not your fault and the reason for it has nothing to do with you. Mom/Dad and I are working together as your parents (or arrangements are being made if they have not been worked out) to make sure you will be able to do things you enjoy because we love you."

CHILDREN OF INTERMEDIATE SCHOOL AGE:

Children, nine to twelve years of age, deal with and have the same concerns as primary school age children. However, children in this age range tend to think of everything in terms of right and wrong, good and bad and may feel they need to take sides if they perceive one parent has hurt the other. It is best to emphasize the separation and divorce are best for all concerned, that the relationship between both parents will continue, that you as parents will try to make sure 'the stuff' they do will continue and that both parents love and care for them and will be there for them.

You should also be prepared to answer questions from your children. Here are some of the most common questions that children ask when they learn of their parents' impending separation, and or, divorce:

- Who is going to move out of the family home, and which child is going to live with them? (This question is often asked if it is not raised by the parents during the announcement.)
- Why is that parent leaving? (Again, this question is often asked if it is not raised by the parents during the announcement.)
- Why have, or why did you stop loving Mommy or Daddy?
- Why will I be living with one parent and not the other?
- Where is the parent that is leaving going to live?
- Will we ever see that parent again? (This is another question often asked if the parents have not discussed custody and access during the announcement.)
- What will happen to us? Children want to know if their routines such as going to school, seeing friends, going to brownies etc, will be affected.
- Won't the parent who is leaving home be sad and lonely?
- When is the parent leaving home?
- Will the parent ever come back?
- Will I be able to see (Mom's/Dad's) grandparents, aunt/uncle/ cousins etc.?

Children want security, consistency and freedom from being involved in the emotional difficulties of their parents. Thus, it is best for parents both during the 'announcement' and after to be aware of how the children are coping with the divorce and be supportive to their needs, stressing the point both parents love them and care for them. Children will usually react to the news of their parent's separation/divorce with a range of emotions from 'shock' or 'shutting down' to sadness and anger/rage. These same emotions may be felt by children later as they cope with the grieving process concerning the break up of their parents and the loss of the 'original family unit'.

However, based from my experience, continually and consistently reinforcing to the children their parents are there for them, and that they are loved and cared for by both parents will greatly enhance children's ability for healthy development.

What seems evident from personal observation of separated and divorced families is that there are two conditions affecting children's adjustment to divorce: the level of conflict in the family preceding, as well as, following a divorce; and, the emotional and socioeconomic circumstances following a divorce. The greater the degree of conflict[6] between parents the more a child has to observe and learn for themselves the values, beliefs and lifestyle of both parents, rather than each parent communicating this to their child. A similar finding is discussed in a study done by Elizabeth Marquardt, published in her book entitled, *Between Two Worlds*[7]. However, she believes low conflict parents should remain married despite the stress and upheaval, as children are better off gaining values and beliefs from their parents in this environment than from a two-parent environment. However, observations of children who witness parental conflict, such as frequent arguing, verbal threats to actual hitting are less well adjusted than children from divorced families. If the parental separation or divorce is expected to be acrimonious and you are expecting a costly legal battle, the emotional fallout and the economic hardship you will experience in the form of anxiety, stress and a general of feeling being unsettled will most likely filter down to your children. Often both parents take a financial hit, however the parent who oversees the household where the children reside usually find it stressful to maintain status quo, if possible. Despite the loss of income this parent is able to maintain parent-child rapport necessary for a child's healthy development.

Experience has shown that fortunately most children not only acquire core values and beliefs from both parents (if allowed consistent and regular contact with both parents after divorce), but learn to adapt to other family dynamics i.e. two separate parental households and thrive, despite the stress and upheaval that is common in

---

[6]*The term 'degree' refers to both intensity – from purposeful silences to arguing, use of profanity and loudness to use of being physical (pushing, slapping, hitting, etc.) and frequency – how often conflict occurs between parents (once or twice a month; once or twice a week; a few times a week; everyday; a few times a day to all the time) Low conflict would for example be arguing, perhaps using some profanity and with few episodes of yelling. An example of high conflict would involve being physical, and or, arguing more than a few times per week.*
[7]*Elizabeth Marquardt.* **Between Two Worlds**. *Three Rivers Press. Sept. 2006*

the early stages of parental divorce. This is borne out in a follow-up study by Constance Ahrons[8] PhD. A group of 180 adult children of divorce was interviewed on the impact of divorce on their lives. What seems clear from Ahron's interviews is that many decisions parent's make when they rearrange the family can make it either better or worse for the children. These are issues we have or will discuss such as: how you tell your children about the separation; the kind of living and custody arrangements you make for the children; how often the children see the non-custodial parent; how they feel about their parent's dating or having new partners; how remarriages are managed; supporting a child's feelings about being in a 'new' family vs. the 'former'; and, how their parent's relate to each other, both during and after marriage. This is especially true, if a parenting partnership is created, guidelines to sort out communication difficulties is established and a semblance parenting plan is followed, such as the ones outlined in this book.

GAINING AN UNDERSTANDING OF HOW YOUR CHILDREN FEEL ABOUT THE DIVORCE

Once the 'announcement' is made, your children will often go through a grief process simultaneously along with their parents. Experiencing this process at the same time may enable you as parents to be sensitive to your children's needs, especially if you have been working on the emotional questions posed in the first chapter, as well as the questions that follow. Working through these questions will better prepare you to be able to respond and support your children's emotional needs. To assist you with examining your children's emotional needs and reactions to your separation, and or, divorce, answer the following questions:

(Note: You will notice certain questions pertain to different stages you will experience during and following the divorce. Some questions you may answer with assurance, others with less certainty, and still others are questions to ponder until the situation arises. You will also notice all of these questions can be discussed with your children. However, some children will not talk about their feelings openly. In this case, it is best to be supportive and let them know you are available and willing to talk about things when they want to do so.)

- How did each child feel about the divorce initially?
- How does each child feel about the divorce now?
- How is each child managing its grief concerning the divorce?
- How does each child feel about you?
- How does each child feel about the other parent?
- What has each child's feeling been toward different living

---

[8] Constance Ahrons PhD. *We're Still Family.* Harper Collins. 2005

arrangements of you and the other parent, change in time spent with them, less money being spent on 'stuff', etc.?

▶ How does each child feel about the custody and access arrangements?

▶ How does each child feel about their parents' dating, or about having a Stepparent?

▶ What is each child's behavior or reaction to friends or others when the subject of divorce is mentioned?

▶ How does each child manage, and or, cope with the transition of visiting with one parent and living with the other?

ANSWERING DIVORCE QUESTIONS

Children need to express their feelings and thoughts about their parents divorce. It cannot be overemphasized that in order for children to feel comfortable about asking their questions, you need to set the groundwork at the time you announce your divorce. By encouraging and welcoming your children to ask their questions promotes and encourages them to express their thoughts or feelings. Answer any questions without expressing anger towards or placing blame on the other parent. Asking questions about what concerns them helps them to cope with the changes to the family that will or have occurred.

Younger children may not be able to express themselves through questions, as they are not aware of what they are feeling, or what feeling they may have means. It is best to let these children know you love and care for them by saying and showing them as often as you can. Parents need to demonstrate consistent care by setting up and maintaining routines. This is true of all children, but especially true of younger children who require consistency and continuity to ensure order in their world. For younger children providing time to color and draw is a positive means for them to express their feelings.

Sit with your younger children and encourage them to draw pictures about things they like to do, things they see i.e. trees, animals etc. Ask them about colors they use, where they saw the tree or animal. You are encouraging and building rapport with your children. Once you have done so you can gently encourage them to draw pictures of friends, siblings, relatives and family. You can ask questions about the colors they use, and about what they like about the picture to gain a sense of how they are feeling about family circumstances. You do not have to explain any details of the divorce, but rather encourage your children through their pictures that you are and will be there for them and that you love and care for them.

If you, and or, the other parent have not encouraged your children to ask questions since your divorce has been announced to them, setting out ground work to encourage and welcome questions will take time and patience. You cannot expect a child to be open and forthcoming with their feelings if you have not. You are going to have to start with a baseline of telling them how much you love them. If you have made any disparaging or flippant remarks about the other parent you will have to stop these comments. Listen to them, and let them have opinions without commenting. Ask general questions about what kind of music they listen to, the clothing kids their ages wear etc. without commenting or being judgmental – simply listen and ask more questions, unless they ask you one. This is usually something like, "Why are you doing this?" If they do ask such a question don't be frivolous or silly about the answer, be honest and tell them you are interested in knowing stuff about them. They may think it strange or weird you are asking (and believe me they will), but slowly and over time you will sense them to be more comfortable, approachable and open to sharing information about their lives. At this point, be cautious and aware not to dump a lot questions about how they feel or think about the divorce on your children. Trying to rush your child to open up about their feelings without first being comfortable to do so may cause you to push your child further away. You can slowly introduce a comment or question such as, "I know our divorce (must have been hard for you, or if you noticed something changed for the child you can state it here) I hope you know we both love and care for you and we want the best for you. I guess it's been hard for you (fill in the blank)." Your child may just say yes or no, or they may make a brief comment. Remember to listen before replying to gain a sense of continuing to explore how they feel, or whether it is best to move on to other matters. Finish the conversation with, "Thanks for letting me know how you feel about this. Knowing this is important to me because I want to make sure you are able to go to school, play with your friends and have fun without worrying about this kind of stuff. So, if you have a question, or you need to talk about anything please come and ask me. I love you." The process of getting children to feel comfortable about asking their questions concerning divorce will take time and a lot of patience.

THE IMPORTANCE OF PARENTS STAYING CONNECTED TO THEIR CHILDREN

A part of a child's development is that they form attachments or bonds to whoever cares for them, usually their mother and father. As they mature, children are able to become more independent developing a positive sense of themselves created from the security of a parent-child bond. Without forming a secure bond through contact and interaction with their parents, a child may become overly anxious at separating from their parents, and in the case of a divorce being apart from one of his parents. In such a circumstance, as a child grows up they will feel insecure and uncertain about them self, and have difficulty forming bonds or attachments with other people or friends. Thus, it is important for children to interact and form bonds with both parents to develop a healthy sense of well-being – feeling loved, wanted and cared for.

Kenny, a boy age ten, did not see his father regularly after his parents divorced. In fact, he never knew when his father would call to talk to him, except for holidays and his birthday, and he rarely ever knew beforehand when he and his father would get together. From conversations with Kenny and from comments from other family members it was apparent Kenny missed spending time with his Dad. What troubled Kenny wasn't that his parents were divorced, but the pain he felt towards his Dad that he did not seem to care about him and had left him. Unfortunately, for Kenny, his Dad has continued sporadic visits with him, and the possible effect is that Kenny probably will to some degree or another have difficulty developing close friendships.

As indicated by this story, how well parents handle the break up and cope with parenting responsibilities can greatly affect a child to some degree, usually in the short term. As in the case above however, boys can be affected the most, feeling abandoned from the loss of their father during divorce if they are at a stage of development where forming a bond with their father is important.

FACING NEGATIVES AND BEING COMMITTED PARENTS IS VALUABLE TO CHILDREN

Parenting prior to separation or divorce may have been difficult because of the uncertainty felt by both parents and children alike. Such a condition may occur as you proceed through the divorce finding yourself uncertain about how to 'be' with your children. The reasons you may be experiencing this vary: you may feel you only want to spend time doing routine activities with your children that feel safe; you may spend less and less time with them as a way to avoid meaningful family interaction that possibly may result in difficult/awkward moments occurring; and, you may find yourself spending far too much time caring for children as a primary care-giver which becomes taxing, which may cause you to feel guilty because you feel are not spending 'quality time' with them. Uncertainty about parenting arises from how you feel or perceive your children are reacting to your being separated; whether you feel or think they are blaming you for the break up of your family; how you can make your children's time conflict-free so you can develop a positive rapport with them; and, how firmly you can discipline and care for your children without them feeling rejected or overwhelmed.

There are no guarantees children won't ask questions and feel at times as if they have had some part in splitting apart their parents. However, the most important role a parent can do is to make sure your children are loved and taken care of by both parents, and that it is ok to love both parents. Both parents need to encourage their children's involvement and communication with the other parent, and with other family members. Children, like parents, can lose their sense of comfort when family dynamics change, so it is important for them to know they are safe. Therefore, it is not uncommon for older children to question and for younger children to feel, "If my Mom and Dad don't love each other anymore, will they stop loving me?"

Parents need to explain, in age related terms, that the love you had for Mom or Dad is different from the love you have for your children and that love will continue. This will reinforce their feelings of being loved and provide them with a sense of comfort.

Despite a change in family dynamic – two parent homes instead of one, children can continue having positive and meaningful parent-child interaction. As a child adapts to two homes, it is important that each home be perceived as a special place. Terms like 'real home' to describe the residence where children reside most of the time and 'other home' to describe the residence where children stay part of the time does not create a connection with their new life. And parents should never ask children to comment on which house they love best, or criticize or judge the children's other home. To do so will make children feel unsafe to talk about not just what they do at the other house, but about their life in general for fear of being ridiculed. Keeping communication open with your children, as well as the other parent as mentioned, is important to creating a conflict-free atmosphere (for details see appendix entitled, *Factors to Developing a Conflict-free Zone..*) for your children that will foster better parent-child rapport. Maintaining communication with the other parent can also remove guessing and assumptions concerning setting consistent limits and boundaries for child.

Observations of divorced families and their parents reveal there are other behaviors that contribute negatively to how children respond to being parented. The benefits of open communication with the other parent are often offset by name-calling, deriding or putting down the other parent directly in front of the children. Telling them that their other parent is a so-and-so will hurt your child, who will feel they are a so-and-so too as they see themselves as being part of that parent. It is best that if you are angry at the other parent about some matter and cannot say anything positive about them it is best not to say anything at all in front of your children, as per the reason just mentioned. Avoiding negative comments about the other parent reduces a child developing a feeling of blaming themselves for contributing to the cause of the divorce. If you blame the other parent for the divorce, and the child identifies as being half the other parent then feelings of being at fault in someway are natural. Such behavior can cause children to view the parent who is making disparaging remarks with resentment, anger and, even a lack of trust by thinking or feeling, 'if they are saying such things about my own parent, what do they say about me or others when we do things they don't like.'

Parents often want to know how children got along with the other parent and what activities they did. It is part of interacting and building a rapport with your children.

When you do ask questions and respond to your child as if you were having a conversation about their day at school or having returned from a friend's house. Too often parents, especially until an established routine of outings with the other parent has occurred, will greet their child with anxiousness which the child senses and is unsure how to respond as they do not want to cause you to feel upset. In turn, instead of realizing their approach, many parents persist with the questions and meet with little forthcoming information from the child, which in turn raises concern in the parent something is 'wrong'. In some situations, parents then ask twenty questions, which further pressures their child into remaining silent about what they did.

If you find yourself in this situation, stop yourself from continuing with your questioning and think of other times when you've asked questions that your child talked to you. Speak calmly and softly as if you were having that conversation. You know your child and if they do not say a lot about 'things' in general they won't being saying a lot about their outing with their parent. Try not to go to a place of suspicion that something is wrong if your child answers with "fine" or "good" to the question, "How was your time with your Mom/Dad?" If you want more detail, you will have to ask more of a specific question. If you know the activity they did ask, "How was the zoo?", or, "What animals did you see at the zoo today, and what ones were your favourite?" By asking specific questions chances are better that you will receive more detail in the response and creating such interaction will help to alleviate your anxious feelings.

To maintain a positive relationship with the other parent you will have to be thoughtful and respectful, and you will have to remain focused on the best interests of your children. You will have to accept that your relationship as a couple has ended and that your relationship as parenting partners will continue for the benefit of your children.

As parenting partners it is best to keep each advised about important matters by not passing messages to one another via your children. It is also extremely important, regardless if you are upset by the other parent's behavior, that you share information needed to attend special events in your child's life so your children are not disappointed by a parent not showing up. (See appendix 'Key Elements Necessary to be Successful Parenting Partners')

Finally, let your children be children. Work through your own emotional process apart from your children –work on the questions and review the emotional process discussed in the first chapters, talk to a friend, see a professional if you are having difficulty resolving personal matters, but do not work through your 'stuff' with your children. Your children may be available to act as your support, as someone you can comfy in, but you must protect and preserve as much of your child's innocence as possible.

COMMENTS AND ILLUSTRATIONS FROM CHILDREN TELL THE STORY OF WHAT THEY THINK AND FEEL ABOUT THEIR PARENTS' DIVORCE

Understanding and recognizing what affects divorce has on children can and does have a profound effect on parent interaction. As part of my work with parents, as a Separation and Divorce Coach and family mediator, parents come to recognize how their behavior affects their children and often make adjustments accordingly to alleviate or cease parental behavior that causes turmoil in their children.

An Australian report released in October 2006[9] by Dr. Jenn McIntosh clearly indicated that parents who were told and shown 'drawings and writings by their own children on how the collapsing marriage affected them... modified their behavior.'

The examples of children's drawings, comments and writing are taken from a group of children, ages seven to eleven years of age, which were brought together to discuss their feelings and thoughts about divorce. They are representative of children's feelings and thoughts whose parents have left them out of the divorce process.

The children were asked, "How does divorce make you feel?" Their answers will probably surprise and shock you: (See the following page)

Here are a few comments from some of the children and their parent's responses:

Todd (age 11): *"It all started when I was 2-3 years old. I'll never forget the day dad said [they] were leaving each other. It made me sad. I also felt it was my fault. There was always something that made me feel something bad was going to happen. He came to me and said he was leaving for a very long time to think about stuff. I really wish my parents had told me what was happening. On this very day it had to happen. He still hasn't come [back]."*

Todd's Mom was very surprised to learn how Todd felt. She said she and her husband thought it was best to spare Todd's feelings by not telling him. She felt awful and said she felt sad she had done this to Todd. However, once she spoke to Todd,

---

[9] *Story written by Caroline Overington in The Australian News on October 11, 2006 on the study conducted by Dr. Jenn McIntosh (D. Psych) for the Australian Institute of Family Studies' October 2006 seminar*

told him the reason for the way it was handled, "because they loved him and did not want him to be hurt", and that he is, "loved and will always be loved by both of them', Todd felt a sense of relief he had never felt before.

Jenny (age 11): *"My Mom and Dad never did anything together and when my Mom wanted to go out my Dad would stay home. I was only four years old when my Mom left. My Dad's excuse was Mom went on vacation but she hasn't come back. I am sad when I think about her and I miss her."*

Dad was both surprised and pleased to learn about what his daughter thought. He said, "I did not realize she still thought of her Mom this way after such a long time because she hasn't asked about her Mom much. I'm glad to know how she feels." Dad was told of the importance to talk to his daughter about what had happened without going into detail, and without attaching blame to her Mom, to empathize about how she was feeling and to let her know how much she is loved and to encourage her to talk about her feelings when she feels sad. Jenny felt better knowing the truth, but needed ongoing support to cope with her feeling about her Mom.

Jason (age 10): *"When I was four I saw my mom and dad yelling at each other a lot. I saw my dad sneaking in the house to get his stuff and he said he would be gone for awhile. He told me stories about mom that are not true. Mom told me stories about dad that are not true also. I was angry at both of them for a long time. They divorced and I only see dad once in a while."*

Mom was embarrassed and shocked that her son remembered what had happened between her and his father. She was also saddened that it affected him the way it did. She said, "I thought I needed to tell him something about why his father was leaving. I didn't realize he knew more than he did, and I didn't mean for him to be hurt by it."

She was told to explain this to her son. Tell him the truth without the details, reinforce the fact she loves him and will continue to do so, and welcome and encourage him to talk about his feelings. Mom was also encouraged to discuss with Jason access with his father. Jason over the next year opened up about talking about his feelings and anger towards his parents and he gradually felt more trusting of others in general.

When asked the question, 'How do you think your parents could help you deal with divorce' the group replied with the following answers:

> Tell us [your divorce] is not our fault
> Help us (encourage) to share our feelings/Don't make us afraid to talk
> Tell us (children) the truth

- Let me phone and visit my Mom/Dad
- Tell me (children) its o.k. to talk and that you (the parent) won't get mad if I do
- Tell me (children) your getting a divorce and give me (children) a reason

As has been described above these are reactions common to most children in response to the breakup of their family. How intensely a child responds to their parents' separation and divorce and breakup of the family will depend on how their parents' interact and the degree of disruption that occurs in the child's life during and especially following the breakup. Families I have worked with show the more parents work together as parenting partners the less the long-term impact of children fearing abandonment by having one parent leaving the home; feeling overwhelmed that the 'family' is gone rather than changed; holding or carrying anger towards one parent because they believe that parent is responsible for the break up; feeling guilty because they believe they are responsible for the breakup of their parents; or, as parents spend less and less time with them they feel isolated, alone, or feel rejected because their parents do not interact with them.

Some children will revert to earlier stages of development i.e. a child that seemed o.k. on their own before copes by clinging to parents. Parents who provide gentle support and reassurance that they love and care for them will ease their children's need to feel secure and safe. Other children may have difficulty sleeping, but maintaining consistent evening and bedtime routines will remedy this occurrence within a few months.

Other common occurrences experienced amongst children is increased aggression seen often in boys as fighting, overt physical rough-housing and play or bullying, and in girls, typically through verbal teasing, bullying, or withdrawal from activities or interaction with peers. School performance can also been effected by hyperactive learning or a lack of attention or focus on studies. Whatever the circumstance, parents need to support their children in continuing to go to school and continue participating in other activities – not isolate them from interacting with others. Parents need to meet regularly with teachers to discuss their children's well-being and need to support and discuss how to handle their feelings about the divorce. The greater the increased interaction and shared parenting done by parents the less likely these reactions will manifest themselves. It is vital that parents act as parenting partners in dealing with their children, especially younger ones, to meet their need for predictability, consistency and reliability.If you are not yet fully convinced, here are some other reasons why the commitment of both parents after separation, and or, divorce is valuable to your children:

How Does Divorce Make You Feel?

Upset!
I don't want them to
get divorced.

Counts
and
Police

Scared

Social Workers
- they help me to
talk.

Scared - they might
take me away and I
won't see my MOM again

SAD - Alone
Only one parent =
not much attention

SAD
Don't get to know
my DAD - MY HISTORY

Uncomfortable. Don't know much
about my D+i.

Upset. Worried
- are we going to be O.K.
Will MY D+i be nice or Mean?
Will I see him again?

Scared - I don't
to know my D+i and
he doesn't get to know
ME

MAD - My Brother acts Like
My DAD.

Embarassed. Mom is always
tight on Money and I can't
Do What Other Kids
Do!

Since Divorce NOBODY'S THE SAME

Dying Plant

plants bleed Too!

- Children who spend consistent times with both parents, not just one, will gradually through continued interaction and rapport building feel more reassured they were not to blame nor experience a sense of guilt that they were somehow responsible for the break up of their parents. Children will be more likely not to experience a sense of loss, nor feel a sense of abandonment.

- Children who have consistent contact with both parents will be less inclined to fantasize, idealize or yearn for a family dynamic that is not based on reality, as both parents through their interaction with them connect them to 'reality'. Children will not feel a pervasive sense of sadness if they spend consistent time with both of their parents.

- A young child can be fearful or anxious when one parent is not involved in their life because they feel if one parent has left so may the other. Seeing both restores a sense of security and continuity of family.

- Children's contact with both parents allows them to develop healthy bonds for exploring relationships on their own later in life.

The information contained in the previous section has been presented as a means to illustrate the importance for you and the other parent to make all parenting decisions with your children in mind. I hope that both of you as parents have been convinced that being involved is worth your effort and time. Having highlighted some of the negative scenarios to avoid the next section focuses on positive behaviors that a parent can do to help strengthen your relationship with your children. (Some of these behaviors have been mentioned previously, but are grouped here for easy reference.)

1. *Safeguard and keep your children away from parental issues.* Children need not be included, nor involved in parental disagreements and disputes. Not involving children in parental matters promotes children feeling secure and comfortable in their life.

2. *Do not be quick to judge, dismiss or correct your child.* Be open to listening without interrupting, even if disagree with what they are saying, and then discuss the issue afterward to ensure they feel safe and comfortable to talk to you.

3. *Setting realistic boundaries and goals for your child.* As a divorced or separated parent we can sometimes feel uncertain about how and what limits we should place on our children – this is normal for any parent to feel – because we do not what to squelch their self esteem in some way, especially in light of having to deal with being a child going through a divorce. However, children need limits to feel secure, but do not set boundaries or goals solely around their having to gain approval or meet your expectations to achieve a goal.

Having a child internalize rules and goals for themselves rather then having to feel they need to seek outside approval avoids a child feeling guilty for having disappointed their parent rather than for not following a rule or achieving a goal.

4. *Practice what you preach.* Hand in hand with the other two behaviors above, try to live your life by example. Most people talk about and demonstrate to their children moderation in their lives. As parents you need to avoid excessive behavior around your children to ensure the sight of seeing their parents out of control does not frighten your children. If children are aware of repetitive excessive behavior on the part of a parent they will develop uncertainty and fear of being in that parent's presence, and may eventually decide they do not want to see that parent at all.

5. *Avoid exposing your child to ridicule through name-calling or put-downs*. Parents should never ridicule or use put-downs to motivate or discipline their children. Moreover, children who experience divorce have particularly sensitive self-images of themselves, and doing so would cause a child to feel unloved, insecure, and perhaps cause them to withdraw from meeting others.

6. *Take time to learn about and play activities your children like to do.* Too often parents swept up in the pace of getting everything that needs to be done, and to fulfill our duty or obligation as parents choose activities – we set the time. the place, even sometimes what they need to wear to do the activity without really finding out if this is the activity they really want to do or not. Ask children what they want to do and listen to their selection because these are activities geared to their age and interests. When stuck for ideas, let children choose activities they want to do. You may be surprised and have fun.

7. *Praise your child and show affection.* Positive attention, positive reinforcement, praise and encouragement are far greater motivators and bolster self-esteem than put-downs, harsh criticisms and corporal punishment. Telling your child that you love them, and when appropriate giving them a hug, a kiss, a pat on the back lets a child feel comforted you love them.

8. *Be open to allowing your child express his feelings.* This is easier said then done, because it requires you to carefully juggle between your ensuring they have respect and authority as a parent from them and that you are the final arbitrator on matters. In addition, you need to balance your behavior to allow acceptance to listen to a child's complaints, angry feelings tempered with positive feelings and thoughts. Allowing a child to feel comfortable expressing themselves enables them to feel comfortable and secure around you and more self-assured outside the home.

How Do You Think Adults Could Help You Deal with Divorce

MORE PROGRAMS FOR KIDS

Tell Kids it's not their fault

KIDS AND ADULTS need PROGRAMS THEY CAN DO TOGETHER!

HELP KIDS SHARE THEIR FEELINGS!
Don't make them afraid to talk.

GIVE CHILDREN MORE COUNSELING
I feel better after talking about it.

Let me visit my Dad.

Tell kids the TRUTH!

"DAD DIDN'T GO ON A TRIP"

Tell kids your getting DIVORCED

TALK to KIDS
LET KIDS PHONE AND VISIT THEIR DAD.

Tell kids it's O.K. to TALK AND THAT YOU WON'T GET MAD IF THEY DO.

Counceling,
Listen to CHILDREN
DON'T JUST BLOW THEM OFF!

The prescription of behaviors outlined is for use in strengthening and developing a closer relationship with your children and complement the ideas to be discussed in the next chapter.

Chapter Four

The Impact of Divorce on Parenting & Parenting after Divorce

▶ Common scenarios divorced parents need to avoid
▶ Dating and having New Partners
▶ Some important parenting practices to follow after Divorce
▶ Key Elements Necessary to be Successful Parenting Partners

COMMON SCENARIOS DIVORCED PARENTS NEED TO AVOID

Parents during the process of separation and divorce find themselves absorbed with adult-to-adult matters. At the same time parents are dealing with the emotions and stress accompanying the loss of their marriage and deciding on how best take action, so too are children absorbed with dealing with their emotions surrounding the loss of 'the family' as they once knew it. The more parents focus on dealing solely with their issues the less time is spent interacting and showing affection to their children.

The more parents withdraw from parenting the greater the need for children to seek a parent's affection. The best method to avoid this situation as divorced parents is to do the groundwork, both the emotional and tangible tasks discussed in chapters one and two of this book and at the end of this chapter. By doing so you will gain sense of control in your lives; create a nurturing and consistent environment for children by sharing parenting responsibilities as much as possible; and, you will take care to avoid the scenarios commonly made by divorced parents, as described in this section.

Jackie and Phil were married for eleven years and their divorce was fairly amicable.

The children, a boy age eight and a girl age ten, live with their mother and Phil took an apartment only twenty minutes walking distance from their house. Both Phil and Jackie loosely agreed upon a parenting arrangement in which each parented the children when the other was working and the children were out of school, as neither had relatives who lived nearby to assist with babysitting. Five months after the divorce Phil was transferred to another office across town and was no longer able to continue with their parenting arrangement. Jackie was feeling stressed by having to reduce shifts she could work to manage the children, and she was feeling pressured to find a reliable babysitter in case of an emergency. It also put a halt to her goal of putting aside money to purchase her own home, which she had been doing when Phil was present.

Within a week of no longer having Phil to share parenting responsibilities Jackie felt overwhelmed and tired, not having enough hours in the day to take care of everything needing her attention. She spent many a restless night while the house was quiet and the children were asleep pondering how to make things better and how she could move on to that next step of owning her own house and doing other things for herself. Jackie even wandered back to her relationship, longing for companionship and the parenting support it had provided.

Jackie's situation of finding herself as the primary care-giver is typical of many a parent within the first year of separation and divorce. Adjusting to a new routine, requiring more time and energy to meet daily demands, and feeling unable to spend quality time with their children can weigh heavy on parents like Jackie. Similarly, parents whose children do not live with them can also feel stressed by not sharing quality time with their children and the loss of participating in the routine of family life.

What is crucial for both parents and their children is how parents approach restructuring of their parenting responsibilities after the break up of their relationship. In Jackie's and Phil's circumstance, having only a loose parenting arrangement that did not outline their roles and responsibilities to each other clearly, nor address contingent actions allowed for one parent having to shoulder most of the parenting. However, had they drawn up a parenting or family plan detailing each others parenting responsibilities and role, Phil probably would have continued to share parenting, and at the very least continued to take an active but different role. Setting out a detailed parenting or family plan alleviates stress, enables parents to spend more quality time with their children and allows their children to adjust to their new family situation.

Here are a number of other commonly occurring parenting situations that you should avoid or change to benefit the family:

▶ Both Bob and Jean felt they were quite involved with their children's lives prior to their divorce. Afterwards, because of their busy schedules interaction with their children seemed confined to discussions around chores, errands and mundane subjects. As this situation became more entrenched as a new way of family life the children became more demanding of the parents, more resistive to saying anything about their lives if asked, and acted disinterested in seeing the parent no longer at home. Bob and Jean had to actively engage with their children to change this situation. They had to actively take an interest in their children's lives by asking specific questions to receive specific answers; listen carefully to what their children said; investigate what was important to their children; ask more specific questions and not be afraid of asking; and, take time to be involved with them. It took both Bob and Jean time and patience for them and their children to get use to this change, but the reward of interacting and bonding with each other was worth the effort.

▶ Dave, Shauna, Paula and Andrew were parents who resented the circumstances of their divorce feeling bitter about their property settlements and financial arrangements, and each talked about their predicament incessantly in front of their children. In doing so, their children desired to spend less and less time with their parent not wanting to feel the negative weight of their parent's resentment. When a few of these parents focused their attention on their children when they were with them and did not bring up matters that should be resolved between adults, both the parent and their children were able to develop healthy parent-child bonds. The parent was able to enjoy their children's company and the children felt comfortable in their parent's presence. Another aspect of this situation, which has previously been discussed, but is worth mentioning because of the negative impact on children, is when parents frequently bad-mouth or ridicule the other parent in front of the children. This has the same result as above, in that children will seek out ways to avoid contact with the negative parent, however the effect upon the children is more severe having a negative impact on their self-image.

▶ Jenny, a custodial parent of two boys, and Dennis, an access parent of a boy and girl, both parented their children the same way. After each of their respective divorces each parent interacted with their children by transferring their disappointment of the failed relationship onto their children, finding aspects of each of their children's character more difficult or exasperating to deal with. Both parents examined their role and avoided imposing severe, arbitrary limits on their children and practiced being accepting and encouraging of them, recognizing their children were adjusting as much as they were to a new family dynamic.

▶ Some parents after their divorce may feel guilty leaving their children with a babysitter, while others may not be able to afford a babysitter. In either case, despite the reason these parents begin to isolate themselves having less contact and interaction with friends etc. outside of their work. These parents may come to resent their children feeling they are responsible for their predicament of shutting them away from spending time with other adults. Donna, a custodial parent of two girls, is typical parent who isolated herself after the divorce. Her time before and after work and on the weekends was an unchanging routine filled with hurried breakfasts, dinners, errands, chores and more chores. Any free time he spent with her children and when she tried to have a babysitter over so she could have time by herself her youngest daughter cried. Donna felt the tension at home after months of what seemed an unending routine to be too much stress and sought out a community group that had a program to share parenting/sitter exchange. (There are many ways you can find and share parenting services – start with neighborhood parents, family and recreation programs or agencies.) She used the program to take time out for herself and to do outings with each of her girls separately so they felt loved and cared for by their parent. Donna felt less burdened by daily demands and discovered spending some time with other adults made her a better parent, as she was able to put family matters into a better perspective rather than feeling overwhelmed by them.

▶ A common situation parents find themselves after they divorce is they become dependent and reliant on their children to fill the vacuum of feeling alone. Tammy had a healthy parent-child relationship with her daughter Stephanie, prior to her divorce to David, whom she had been married to for twelve years. Tammy and Stephanie had built a positive bond over the past few years as they spent ten to fifteen hours a week together involved in sports -Tammy was manager of Stephanie's soccer team and coach of her field hockey team. Stephanie's relationship with her father was also positive and after the divorce the two spent a few weeknights and every other weekend together. The rest of time away from school was spent with her mother. However, after a few months (usually within a year of the divorce in most situations such as this) Tammy began to interfere with Stephanie's visits with her father. When David would call to arrange a visit Tammy would tell him Stephanie was busy or she wouldn't be able to visit him for the entire weekend because of other planned arrangements. Stephanie also began to cancel visits with her father, afraid to leave her mother alone by herself. The visits became so disrupted David was forced to take the matter to court to resolve his being able to see Stephanie. In such matters as this, a family counselor is needed to assist Tammy and Stephanie to recognize and reorganize their roles as parent and child, while at the same time Stephanie's access with her father should be resumed to ensure she feels safe and secure reestablishing a positive relationship with her other parent too.

If any one of these signs are present in a parent-child relationship this may indicate that the parent may depend too much on their children and should avoid involving the children in such action, or they should contact a family counselor to assist them to stopping such behavior[10]:

▶ Constantly relying on the oldest child to provide most of the care for younger siblings

▶ Continually relying on the oldest child or the children themselves to cook meals and do chores etc. to the point doing these activities interfere with their doing schoolwork or social activities

▶ Describing financial troubles

▶ Asking children for their permission to go on dates

▶ Providing details of the dates

▶ Sharing intimate details about the marriage and divorce

Discussing or sharing details on their sexual activity

▶ Trying to alleviate their loneliness or depression by keeping the children home from school

▶ Trying or talking children out of visiting with the other parent

▶ Constantly complaining to their children about "how hard life is'

Recognizing and understanding how to eliminate or avoid these situations while parenting your children will enhance your chances of establishing a healthy par-

---

[10] *How to Help Your Child Overcome Your Divorce.* P. 93

ent-child bond. Making time for your self, finding ways and providing opportunities to interact with other adults, and allowing your children to explore their world with friends and their other parent will make your children more receptive to wanting to be apart of a family. Creating such a lifestyle for yourself will make you that much more effective as a parent providing you with an ever-wider perspective and outlook by which you can interpret and deal with your children's behavior and needs. Your children in such an environment will feel nurtured and secure being allowed to be themselves fee of the distractions of adult matters.

MOVING ON

Separating feelings such as anger, blame, guilt or grief etc. regarding your past relationship from the practicalities of raising your children and continuing a relationship as parenting partners (See next chapter for details.) will enable you to distance yourself from your past relationship, a step towards moving on with your life beyond the divorce.

Creating a social life for yourself is crucial to your vitality as an adult, as well as a parent. This means more than reacquainting yourself with old relationships or searching for a new relationship. Often couples that knew you as part of a couple before the divorce find it awkward involving you in gatherings with other couples.

It is best to feel grounded and have a sense of who you are as an individual before seeking out another relationship. You need to permit yourself to learn new skills, pursue school, career, hobbies, or explore a passion that you didn't have time when you were in a relationship. However, for some, especially people who are shy or have focused their energy on their family pursuing social activities aside from family may be not be so easy. No matter what your circumstance the easiest and safest way is to start to enlarge your social circle and activities by making good use of the interests, friends and family you have available to you. You are more apt to meet people similar to yourself, with similar interests in connection to people you already know. Once you have gained confidence and you can then expand your social circle.

DATING

Once you have given yourself time to reflect and deal with some or many of the issues from your previous relationship and feel more settled with who you are you may wish to date. Some people want and are able to start rebuilding their lives quickly and look for new opportunities to form intimate relationships, while for others for various reasons this will not be an option. They may choose to wait for their children to be grown; they do not want to be hurt again; they do not want another person coming into their life and telling them how to live; or, because they do not want their family to be hurt, or they themselves are not ready to move forward in their life signal to their children, friends and former partner that the people they are dating are just friends.

Dating as a separated or divorced adult can seem intimidating and confusing because of age, your concept on relationships, perception towards intimacy/sex and having a family to keep in mind. Your children may even dissuade you from dating because of their lingering fantasy they have of you and their other parent could someday reunite, or they may feel you are betraying their concept that dating after 'the relationship you had family with' is not right. Whatever the case, your dating marks another transition for your children that you are moving on in your life. Be open and talk to your children about your plans to date so there is no illusion that you and their other parent will reunite and enable your children to readjust to seeing you with someone else.

Dating is a time you can learn as much about yourself through interacting with others. It is an activity that demonstrates to a parent that they need to build a life outside their family and that there children need to do the same so that neither becomes too dependent on the other. Most divorced people do date again and eventually remarry or re-partner.

Here are some points to keep in mind about dating[11]:

> Do not think of dating solely as a means to find a new partner

> Be yourself and be age appropriate

> Do not go on a date and vent sharing your anger and hurt with the other person

> If your former partner begins to date do not vent your hurt or anger at your children

> Do not hide your dating from your children

> Let your children know about your date in a reassuring manner without providing a lot of information they do not need to know. For example tell them about what activity you are doing i.e. dinner, movie etc., that the person looking after you has the phone number of how to get a hold of you in case of an emergency, and the time you will be home. If it is after the children's bedtimes let them know you will check in on them when you get home. This kind of information lets your children know you have not forgotten about them, they can take comfort

---

[11] *Helping Your Child Through Your Divorce. pp.108 - 110*

in knowing your whereabouts and that you will be returning and not abandoning them.

▶ Let common sense be your guide in sexual matters. Do not engage in sexual activity in front of your children or bring home a date to spend the night with you

▶ Do not engage in a succession of short-term, intense relationships

▶ Be careful about dating and engaging in sexual activities before your divorce is final. If your former partner is suing you for custody of the children, such activity can be used as negotiating leverage against you.

▶ Do not think of your dates as stand-in-parents. You alone are responsible for the care and discipline of your children

▶ Do not use your dating activities as a means for hurting your former partner or proving to them that you are sexually active

▶ Never encourage your children to report on their other parent's dating activities to you. Your former partner has a right to privacy and your children do not need to be put in a position of tattle tallying

▶ If your former partner is dating someone steadily do not turn your children against that person when they all to be getting along well together. Keep in mind no one can ever replace a parent in a child's heart.

Integrating your adult personal life with your life as a family member and parenting partner is the key to how you and your children will overcome the effects of divorce and move beyond it. An essential tool of benefit to both parents, as parenting partners, and children is the parenting or family plan, components of which are highlighted in the next chapter.

NEW PARTNERS

A great majority of parents re-partner sooner or later, and it will become increasingly likely that the two households your children now belong to or are getting use to will contain people who were not part of the original family.

The introduction of a new partner depends a great deal on *timing*. Both parents should spend time with their children after the separation and long enough afterward to develop a strong parent-child bond and routine at each household before introducing new partners. Too many adjustments all at once can be overwhelming for children.

Introducing a new 'special' person into your children's lives, especially if the children know this person before your marriage or relationship ended will more likely than not result in that person being viewed as the reason for the breakup. The parent that introduces this 'special' person will also be blamed for causing the split up, and both the parent and the special person will be resented for doing so.

Having a 'special' new partner will also spark strong emotions in your children:

- Resentment – directed at both parents (even if the other parent did not know) for allowing this affair to occur, and for the embarrassment of having the relationship known to family and friends etc.

- Jealousy – having to now share their time with their parent with someone else

- Betrayal – having a relationship with this person who is seen as having sabotaged the family

- Anger – for the change of circumstances to the family, and at one or both parents for not keeping the family together

The intensity of these emotions can be avoided if you introduce this new 'special' partner after you have established a strong relationship with your children and they are comfortable about going between two households.

The following guidelines should help insure a positive introduction and ease the transition of having a new person involved in their parent's, as well as their lives:

- Wait until you have a solid parent-child relationship, and are comfortable adjusting between two households

- Be gradual in introducing your new partner to your children. In other words, when your new partner and children are together do not be so absorbed in your new partner that your children feel neglected. This will cause resentment and create jealousy.

- Be sensitive to listening to your children's comments and how they feel about your new relationship. Adjusting to seeing a new person other than their other parent goes against their fantasies of 'family' and seeing their parents together. It will take time for children to make adjustments. Reassure your children that the new partner is not more important to you then they are.

- Be open and honest with your children about your uncertainties and direction of your relationship, so they feel included, and do not feel uncertain about what is going to happen to their relationship with you when you separated from their other parent. Be open and honest to your new partner about your relationship with your children to avoid surprises or assumptions being made about your new relationship in relation to the children.

▶ Be diplomatic and do not encourage your new partner to take on a parenting role, as it will cause friction between the new partner and your children and cause tension for you in mediating situations

▶ Be thoughtful or mindful of your children and do not introduce or involve any new partner until they become 'significant' and will remain in your life for sometime.

Here are a number of questions you need to address before introducing your children to a new partner:

1. Do you have a solid parent-child relationship with your children? And, are they comfortable with moving between two households? If the answer is yes to both, then introducing a new partner will be easier.

2. Have you broached the subject of dating and have another person in your life with your children? Listening to and discussing their concerns will prepare and allow them to feel more comfortable discussing concerns later when a new partner or step-parent enters their lives.

3. How is your ex-partner or spouse likely to react to your having a new partner? As a courtesy, you should tell them about your new partner before introducing your children, so they can get used to the idea. The children should not be the ones who tell their parent about their other parent's new partner.

4. Have you set out a plan to introduce the children to your new partner? Have you discussed your children with your new partner, and their role then and in the future? Avoid overt displays of affection with your new partner during the initial meetings with the children, and do not have a new partner sleep with you shortly after introducing the children to your new partner and they are staying over. Doing so will further complicate sorting out their image of 'family'.

Children can and do cope surprisingly well with new relationships provided that their lives are not overwhelmed; that they feel part of being a 'family'; that their parents are tolerant and thoughtful of their child's needs, and are respectful of maintaining a parent-child relationship.

Children should be encouraged to accept that parents have needs of love, intimacy and compassion that are separate from their children. Of course, you have the right to have relationships, except you also have an obligation to consider your children and their feelings. In is interesting to note, that children are often relieved when both parents have relationships, as things seem somehow fair or balanced.

SOME IMPORTANT PARENTING PRACTICES TO FOLLOW AFTER YOUR DIVORCE
THE IMPORTANCE OF PARENTS MAINTAINING CONTACT WITH THEIR CHILDREN

It cannot be over emphasized the importance of parents maintaining contact with their children during the separation. In other words, the parent who left the family home needs to stay in contact via phone calls and see their children as soon as possible after the separation. Likewise, it is equally important for the parent residing with the children to purposefully spend time and interact with their children. Many children become anxious when a parent moves out of the home.

Once separated, parents' cannot become focused solely on dealing with spousal issues and must provide time to interact with their children to meet their needs to feel safe, secure and loved. Staying in contact and maintaining parent-child interaction alleviates a child's feeling and thought that they may be to blame for their parent's breakup, and spending time with them reassures them that you love and care for them. Consistent and regular interaction provides a child with a sense of stability and assurance they will have a relationship with their parents.

Paul and Rhonda was a couple that I met with to discuss parenting after divorce.

One of the concerns each brought up to me was the way the children were now feeling about their Dad having left and how they would feel about seeing him, as it had been almost ten weeks since he last saw the children – the day when he left the family home. As I talked to both of them it became clear that neither Dad nor Mom had any meaningful interaction with their children – Mom, only through giving daily direction to maintain household chores, homework and driving to scheduled appointments, and Dad, had no contact at all. When the discussion focused on what each of them felt or believed what the children were actually feeling about their separation, both realized they did not really know how any of their children were thinking or feeling, or how it was having an impact on them. I discussed with both of them, having Rhonda set up a time I could meet the children to discuss their feeling about their parents' separation. After speaking with the children I had a meeting with Mom and Dad to discuss what they had said. All three children I told Paul and Rhonda felt insecure about feeling loved by them; felt uncertain that they were not somehow responsible for causing the demise of their relationship; and, they were not sure about what was going to happen between their parents and themselves. To begin to minimize the children's uncertainty about a relationship with their parents an access schedule with their Dad was set up and a schedule of times Mom could interact with the children. Next, to alleviate feelings of insecurity around feeling unloved and to reduce their feeling that they were somehow responsible for their parents' breakup a meeting was arranged with the three children and both parents. The children heard a united voice from their parents that they were loved by them both, that they were not responsible in any way for their breakup and that both of them recognized their relationship with their children was very important to each of them and they wanted to be with and do things more often with each of them together and separately. To ensure this happened days and times were set up for each child to spend with each parent. Within a few months the scheduled days and times had changed to fit in with everyone's routine, however the emotional turmoil and uncertainty was gone and both parents and children were feeling secure in knowing they had a healthy parent-child relationship.

What the above scenario also highlights, is that if the parent who has the children, *encourages the children to develop a positive relationship* with the other parent, the children would feel secure and loved having a parent-child relationship with that parent continue. If a child is encouraged to see their other parent a schedule of regular visits should be planned for or arranged. Ongoing contact via telephone, e-mail and visits will allow a child to feel loved and cared for by both parents – by the parent they live with because they encourage visits and care about the child's need to see the other parent, and by the other parent for being a part of their life.

KEEPING YOUR WORD

Parents need to keep their promises to their children in order to build trust with them. They need to count on both parents to feel secure that the world will not crumble around them.

Heather age eight, and her brother Bobby, age six, saw there other parent twice a week for a few hours each visit. The parent they lived with encouraged them to see their other parent. As the other parent's work increased the children spoke less and less to them on the phone and they began to show up for visits later and drop the children off sooner than the expected time the visit was to end. Presents or promises to bring a toy, or do an activity were not kept, until the children's anticipation of promises being kept turned to caution and guarded hope, to finally disappointment then disbelief and trust in their other parent. Such behavior by a parent undermines a child's security and they lose trust in that parent which is difficult to rebuild. Children may even feel rejected by that parent if such behavior persisted. Therefore, if promises cannot be kept, provide a simple explanation to reassure the children it is not because of something they have done. If possible, reschedule or plan to make up the visit, obtain a gift, or do an activity – whatever promise was not kept. In addition, if a parent needs to make a change or cancel plans for a visit, call as soon as possible before the visit to allow for alternative plans to be made.

AVOID DISCUSSING ANY SPOUSAL OR PARENTAL ISSUE YOU ARE IN DISAGREEMENT IN FRONT OF THE CHILDREN.

It is apparent from comments made by children I talk with that listening to their parents' disagreements about money, custody, visits etc. causes a child to feel unsettled and confused. As one child said, "Mom tells me one thing... and I hear another thing... from my Dad. It's confusing at times and I don't know who to believe." Arrange and set up times to meet or call your former partner, especially following the separation because there is usually lots of details that need to be discussed and reworked to fit both your schedules, meet your needs and those of your children. E-mail only questions and discuss only the issues that need to be resolved. AVOID any personal comments, name-calling or anything derogatory. Stay focused on the subject and discuss the issue as it currently affects you or will in the future.

KEEP SPOUSAL AND COUPLE ISSUES SEPARATE FROM PARENTING

Too often I have witnessed divorced parents debate over what is in the best interest of their child. In some of these situations, one parent often feels the other parent is forcing them to comply with standards for their child that are unnecessary, unreasonable or are truly not in their child's best interest. In many of these incidents were parents do not come to some mutual arrangement or agreement regarding an issue feelings of resentment, anger, frustration towards their former partner my effect their parenting.

A couple came into to see me regarding a number of issues, a number of them to do with financial issues, and one of which was, should their child continue the use of a prescribed drug used supposedly to aid in his ability to concentrate. Both parents agreed the drug had worked well for their son while he was in grade school.

The issue now was over the effectiveness and long-term effect on their child taking the drug while going through puberty. Both presented their opinion based on research and concerns they had about each other's research. However, the matter could not be resolved and one parent told the other that their child would continue to take the prescribed drug. The other issues were only partially resolved and were to be discussed again a few months later.

The child alternated living with each parent every two weeks. The other parent decided that during the time the child was with them they would not be on the prescribed drug. This continued into the school year for about six weeks before they were asked to come to the school. The child's teacher informed them she had noticed wide swings in behavior about every two weeks or so and was concerned by the behavior. The one parent explained what they had done and the other parent became furious and threatened to go back to court for causing harm to their child.

The parent explained they felt the other parent was not listening and believed the other parent refused to look at alternatives in the best interests of their child, because of not having resolved the other issues. The issue after lengthy discussion was resolved and their child was prescribed a less evasive but just as effective drug.

It is best to not make assumptions and keep spousal and couple issues separate from parenting issues to ensure you as parents work cooperatively together.

NOTIFY THE OTHER PARENT IN THE EVENT OF AN EMERGENCY

If a health issue occurs i.e. a child has an asthma attack, or there is a medical emergency i.e. your child breaks their arm contact the other parent as quickly as possible. First and foremost, a child who is feeling frightened and upset by the event or accident wants to have both their parents there to care and reassure them they are ok. The parent whose care the child was in at the time of the event or accident needs to contact the other parent as soon as possible to reassure them their child is ok. The sooner the better is the optimum action to take to avoid the other parent's imagination from running rampant with negative thoughts if they found out later.

A word of caution, to the other parent, once you are told of the emergency, do not rush to your child and make any comment negative or otherwise to that parent in front of child. Focus on them and speak privately with that parent later.

As you have read in this chapter there are many behaviors to avoid and do as a parent that can affect your ability to have a positive influence on your child and create a healthy parent-child bond. The key is to focus your attention on what you can do now and not dwell on the past.

KEY ELEMENTS NECESSARY TO BE SUCCESSFUL PARENTING PARTNERS

1. Stop blaming the other parent or yourself for what happened in the past. Deal with issues in the present and look to the future and do not dwell on the past, as it cannot be relived.

2. Be mindful and respectful of your child's need to have two parents involved in their life, and make allowances to ensure your child can be with the other parent.

3. To avoid bringing up unresolved spousal issues keep discussions with the other parent to issues pertaining to your children.

4. Stay focused in the present on your child's needs and do so from now on.

5. Make every effort to defuse tension, to negotiate and compromise and to resolve issues by being flexible, so that your children can live without stress and anxiety of being caught between their feuding parents.

6. If you cannot work with the other parent amiably, then work together as business partners sharing parenting responsibilities to provide your child with a nurturing and conflict-free an environment as possible. (See chapter eight appendices for further details.)

Chapter Five

Parenting Plans

You may be surprised to learn the first important step in creating a parenting plan begins when you and the other parent strategize and set out how to make the 'announcement'(as discussed in chapter three) concerning your separation/divorce to your children, demonstrating that despite remaining together as a couple you are working together as parents.

The information gathered from questions and tasks you have reviewed from the first two chapters will be of assistance in drafting a parenting plan the will not only meet the needs of both parents, but will especially address the needs of your children. Here are a number of goals you need to keep in mind to draft a successful parenting plan:

- Continue your work on moving through the divorce process.
- Forgive yourself, the other parent and let go of your anger.
- Maintain a sense of family by constructing a vision that enables your children to feel comfortable being in two parental homes. A parenting plan should allow both parents to have meaningful and positive interaction with their children. Make new rules for how your two households will be connected. For example, parents can be consistent at setting bedtimes on school nights and weekends; wake up times on school days; the amount of TV and computer game playing children can do; boundary setting; personal hygiene routines; school/homework routines; and, scheduling extra-curricular activities.
- Be open-minded – When you agree on an issue agree -do not put so many conditions on an issue that it will fail. Think outside the box regarding future matters.
- Compromise to meet children's needs – it is in everyone's, especially your children's best interest to keep your family a

family. Do not become trapped by 'I did this, they should do that'; or, 'I conceded this, you should concede that'. Such attitudes benefit no one especially your children who will quickly sense the awkwardness and tension of implementing a plan based on this arrangement.

▶ Use common sense – When planning be patient and sympathetic to the other person's point of view, not just your own.

▶ Keep in mind children need time to adjust to issues you and the other parent may agree upon. You may need to slow down implementing ideas to allow children to adjust to the process.

▶ *Keep in mind* your children have a need to see both parents.

▶ If possible, cooperate with the other parent for the sake of your children.

▶ Establish a family or parenting plan with clear rules.

▶ Make allowances for your child's family to expand to include step family.

Repeated observation of families has taught me this lesson over and over again:

It is better to have too much information covered in the plan then not enough.

Despite valid reasons which I have heard from parents, such as, "The other partner and I have agreed to…, or are amiable with this or that issue so we don't have to worry about or address this matter." *Write it Down,* circumstances change and often do. Be prepared for and do not be surprised by change. Change is the one constant you can count on as children grow.

Paul and Judy upon separating both agreed they wanted their children to attend the Sunday school at the neighbourhood church until their thirteenth birthday. It was a spoken agreement that they never formalized and two years after their divorce the pastor at the church left and a new school committee was formed. Both parents did not like the new Sunday school lessons that were being taught to their children, but Paul felt taking the children away from the school they knew and children they played with would be too unsettling for them. Judy disagreed. A heated dispute ensued which was finally resolved through mediation, and one that they almost went to court.

Had Paul and Judy not only discussed but had written their agreement down, along with how they would resolve the issue if a change occurred six weeks of intense arguing and frustration would probably not have occurred, nor affected their children who were caught up in the turmoil that resulted from their dispute.

So if Paul and Judy, as with other parents, plan for and write down ways too deal with or resolve changes will too much information stifle or bog down how a parent can parent?

Addressing issues and building contingences perform a number of functions:

1. Clarity – both parents (and children) will know what to expect

2. Balances control – in cases, where one parent seems to have been more controlling a parenting plan removes control to a more equitable agreed upon plan

3. Detailed Plans – when implemented and used effectively will actually build trust between both parents. This point can not be stressed enough. Re-establishing trust, building confidence that both parents can follow through and develop a relationship heightens the possibility that any changes that need to be done to the parenting plan can be seamless. In turn, the more solid a plan the better a parenting partnership will be established and the more effective both of you as parents will be in addressing and meeting the needs of your children.

CUSTODY

The issue of custody to decide what living arrangement is best for their children can cause some parents to become gladiators fighting for what each believes is their right as a parent. Assumptions about who has the right can be based on societal pressures caused by social stigma which will cause a mother to feel she is the best choice to have custody of their children; and, a father out of guilt, believing he has left his children too long to fend for themselves may want to protect his children by seeking custody. Such a possessive attitude of being the right parent can also stem from a parent feeling threatened that he or she will be controlled by the other parent or will lose their children. Such circumstances often result in custody being decided by a court with some or little direct input from the parents themselves concerning the decision. For others, deciding custody can paralyze them to not act out of fear, confusion, or not wanting to hurt the other parent. In many of these situations parents choose mediation instead of court, as a mediator helps to facilitate the parents' discussion and their resolution concerning custody. Still, others see their former partner as a good parent and take a middle of the road approach to deciding custody, drafting an outline themselves, or fine tuning it through mediation before submitting it to court. Regardless of how parents settle this issue, deciding custody of your children stirs up emotions within every parent as to what they were like: before separation/divorce; perhaps what kind of parent they are now; and, how they see them self as parent in the future.

For some parents, sharing parenting responsibilities with the children's other parent is a sensitive and painful thing to do. Yet sharing your children is one of the best ways you as parents can show your love to your children. For many parents the concept of sharing parenting is hard to imagine given they had a hard time getting along with the other person when they were partners. However, sharing parenting responsibilities does not require each parent to be friends, or like each other. What is required is that you and the other children's parent work together cooperatively regarding your children, akin to a relationship between business partners.

Go back and review the answers to questions posed in chapter one on your role as a parent. These answers should provide you with a perspective as to how you see yourself parenting which you can then use to best address what custody arrangement would be best for your children.

Listed below are several alternatives to the decision of who should have custody of your children:

- Mother has custody
- Father has custody
- Parents share custody described legally as joint custody and guardianship
- Parents jointly share or split physical custody i.e. children spend half the year with one parent and then the other half of the year with the other, or three days with one parent and four days with the other. (see next section)
- Children are divided – boys go with their father, and girls go with their mother.
- Neither parent has custody – the children live with relatives, foster parent, godparents etc.
- A parent through consent of the other parent or by order of the court because of mental or physical illness, drug dependency, mental/physical abuse, extreme neglect, etc.

Here are others questions to assist you with your decision:

Which alternatives would be best for you? Which alternative would be best for you as a parent? Are they the same? What is the reason for the difference, if any? Which custody arrangement would be best for your children in relation to your answers above? If you want custody of your children, what are your reasons? Is it solely to gain an identity as a parent; out of fear of being criticized for not having custody; out of anger and spite to get back at the other parent; because you believe you are the better parent able to look after the children. Remember that if you believe the other parent will contest custody for one of these reasons or any other, such a dispute can have a harmful effect on your children by putting them in the middle of your fight, so weigh the effects contesting custody with have on your children and decide whether putting your children through such trauma will be worth your gaining custody. You may also feel even though you are not able to live with your partner, nor agree with them as an adult, the other person is a good parent and for the sake of the children you believe sharing parenting is possible? If you decide on an alternative other than sharing parenting, will you be willing to accept that role as a parent, and how will you deal with any adverse criticism you may receive? As children are sensitive and can pick up on your state or mood and how you feel about something, you should keep in mind that the decision that is best for you will also be the best for your children. So if you decide, for example, you want sole custody of children when this is really what you do not want, it is more than likely your children will sense this.

SHARED PARENTING, JOINT CUSTODY AND JOINT GUARDIANSHIP

A common misconception amongst separating or divorcing parents is that if one parent receives sole custody, they won't ever have to deal with their children's other parent again. Holding onto such a belief will only compound parenting issues not resolve them. In reality, parents will have to deal with each other concerning parenting issues as long as they and their children are alive. Another common misconception concerns the meaning of joint custody – a belief that joint custody means fifty-fifty sharing of children's time between parents.

Joint custody, as a legal term, means that both parents share responsibility and authority with respect to their children. Where both parents share responsibility and authority, both parents have the right to make major decisions about their children's life, e.g. health, education, recreation and welfare. This is known as *joint-legal custody*. In practice, this means both parents discuss and make decisions together that affect their children's lives. Another term pertaining to joint custody is *Joint-physical custody* which means the children will live with each parent for specified amounts of time according to the plan outlined by the parents. Such a plan should consider what is in each child's best interest according to their age, school schedules and recreation activities, their relationship with friends and relatives, and the parent's work schedule and availability.

In practice, joint custody or any form of custody, does not mean that both parents share fifty–fifty financial support for their children. If one parent earns more than the other parent, that parent usually contributes more toward their children's support. The deciding issue is whether that parent has the ability to pay or contribute more financially than the other parent, not whether they have the children fifty percent of the time.

Sharing custody has several advantages than other forms of custody:

1. It allows parents the opportunity to continue to have significant responsibility in raising their children and to remain involved in their children's lives.

2. A shared-custody arrangement ensures that one parent will not be overburdened and burned out from having the sole responsibility of caring and meeting the needs of their children. In a shared parenting arrangement, each parent has significant amounts of time with and without their children, which enables them to recharge themselves personally, while at other times maintain and build close relationships with their children.

3. Shared custody arrangements encourage children to thrive by allowing them to have close and continuous contact with both parents. In situations, where children feel comfortable and secure with their relationship with their parents, children seem as I have observed, to readily adapt to going between two homes without much disruption.

4. Parents who share custody, as I have witnessed, find themselves less often embroiled in power struggles and are more willing to settle issues expediently and with little fall-out. This is true for any parenting couple, even divorcing parents who do not like each other. In this, as in any other instance where parents do not like one another, parents can still parent cooperatively by treating one another respectfully as they would a business partner. Furthermore, experience has shown parents who have shared custody arrangements entered into court battles or returned to court to resolve parenting issues.

PRACTICAL ASPECTS OF A PLAN

A parenting or family plan is a formal agreement or statement of how the needs of the children are going to be met after separation and divorce. A parenting plan is a useful tool that outlines social, recreation, medical and educational implications for each child in a formal custody arrangement. This means parents agree upon issues that may seem obvious, draft plans to accommodate the possibility of changes, and set out contingencies to prepare and make allowances for the uncertainties and changes that will occur in their children's lives.

Whatever custody arrangement you decide, a complete parenting plan should have the children's best interests and needs in mind, as well as address parent's needs, preferences and schedules. The following elements should be considered when making a plan:

> *Terminology* –Parents should only use and mutually agree to terminology both understand to avoid miscommunication. In other words, use language that you both agree will work and last. Use of words such as 'standard', 'reasonable', or 'in the best

interests of' are legal terms used as indicators for what is 'good or fair for children'. Terms such as these may not be useful or practical in a parenting plan unless both parents understand what they imply. (See sample outlines of parenting plans at the back of this book.)

▶ *Access* – Remember to decide this from what works best for your children. The details to be discussed include: date, times, how pick up and drop off will occur, and frequency or schedule of visits should be outlined. Details how to get a hold of the other parent in case of cancellation by either parent, plus a plan for make up times should be drafted, as well as, including any other details particular to your circumstance. This should include how and when judgment call will be made, and how the other parent might still have contact with the sick child. (Also see chapter six concerning supervised access.) Note: Infants and young children should see and spend time with both parents frequently. Toddlers and preschoolers need to see a non-custodial parent more often than older children, as a fortnight, and even a week to these children will feel like a very long time to them.

▶ *Venue* – Ensure that the non-custodial home is child-friendly and that children have access to toys and games that are age appropriate. Both parents should allow children to borrow and take toys, games, stuffed animals etc. between both homes to maintain a child's sense of comfort and security. A child's sleeping quarters should be separate from the parent's when children have overnight stays. It is fine during initial visits if children stay over at a relative's home for overnight visits, if this is done a few times while the non-custodial parent is settling into a new residence. However, continuing such arrangements does not provide for consistency and will be confusing when the overnight stays move to their parent's residence. Children should also feel comfortable and encouraged to contact their other parent by e-mail and phone calls.

▶ *Duration* – How to share and divide up the role of parenting. How many hours and days children spend with each parent depends on their age and needs. Very young children and infants initially require shorter more frequent contact with both parents to develop attachment and bonding, including consistent routine. Plans set up by parents that closely follow existing routines will greatly benefit children minimizing disruption to their children's development. This should include after-school provisions and weekends.

▶ *Build* flexibility *into the plan and draw up provisions to account for changes.* i.e. School-age children and adolescents should be able to attend school functions and take part in extra-curriculum activities.

▶ *The plan should be reviewed as children age, and or, if any modifications or changes need to be made to meet their needs.*

▶ *Do not pressure yourself or the other parent to make unreasonable or undoable concessions to your work schedules in an attempt to make your family plan work* – Parents' work schedules must be accommodated.

▶ *All the children all the time see their other parent during access* – The all–together principle that all the children at the same time visit with their other parent ensures no one misses out on time and avoids thoughts of favouritism by siblings, but the opposite can be true too. There is no doubt a fourteen year old and an eight-year old may not want to hang out together and would rather do activities appropriate to their age. So too might an eleven year old and a nine year old may want to have separate 'unique' outings with each parent. Arranging some separate time with each child is healthy, but should be discussed with the children as a group to let them know of this arrangement so no child feels left out and the activity planned for each child is enjoyable and special to each of them.

▶ *Special Days:* Where and how will your children spend holidays and who will take care of them when they are not in school? If you both work who will deal with the sick child? These include children's and parent birthdays, school holidays including Winter and Spring breaks plus school days, professional development days, sick days, Father's/Mother's Day, important religious holidays, both maternal and paternal family events, children's sports and cultural events. Be willing to compromise and open-minded to looking at the significance a special day may have to the other parent and to your child. Be flexible in sharing days if splitting days can be reasonable, realistic and not overly disruptive to the flow of the special day. For instance, if your children's maternal and paternal grandparents who live two hours from each other were having Christmas dinner on the same day it would be unreasonable, unrealistic and overly disruptive to eat at one place and then pack up and travel to another for yet another meal. Information gathered from parents and children themselves reveals most children would rather celebrate an event twice rather than feeling rushed just so they can celebrate an event with everyone. Make sure you also discuss Summer plans to make sure neither parent makes assumptions about either's expectations and to ensure both parents are aware of their children's plans.

▶ *Letting children decide which parent they want to live with* – Asking a child which parent they would prefer to live with would in most circumstances cause a child to feel caught in the middle and cause a them great distress having to choose between two parents they love. The deciding factor as to which parent a child should live with should always be "What is in the best interest of the child?" If you and the other parent are in a disagreement over this issue seeing a counselor or mediator would be advisable before proceeding to court.

There is an exception: Older children/adolescents may express a desire to live with one parent. There may be a number of reasons for this, including wanting the opportunity to further develop a relationship with that parent, or this may be a way for this child to express part of their development of wanting to be independent by making their own decision. Sometimes an adolescent will use threats or emotional blackmail to try and persuade a parent they want to go live with their other parent. This behaviour should not be tolerated, and if possible, both parents should meet to discuss their child's behaviour. This discussion should also include setting a time both can meet together with their child to let them know their behaviour is not acceptable, and discuss a consequence with the child if it continues. If you, and or, the other parent are not able to resolve this behaviour with your child it would be best to see a counselor to assist in dealing with this situation. However, in most situations if a child expresses a desire to live with the other parent look at the request from "what is the child's best interest?" If this occurs here are a few questions to ask yourself:

1. Am I listening and being open to communicating with my child? Am I reflecting on my own feelings, rather than finding out about their request?

2. What is the reason my child wants to live with their other parent? Because of the two reasons mentioned above, or is this different from what I really believe? Possibly, because of problems you and your child are having in your relationship, or because they want to escape problems with friends or school? If so, you need to speak with your child again.

▶ *Let children decide whether they want to visit their other parent or not* – It is best not to contemplate this idea, as parents should never risk putting their children in a position of having to choose between one parent at the expense of time with the other parent. Parents planning outings with their other parent reassures children that they still are part of a family.

Parents can present children with choices as to what activity they would like to do, or the time they would like to do an activity provided both parents know and have agreed to these alternatives.

▶ *Both parents should have the opportunity to care for their children before a third party i.e. babysitter is brought in to care your children:* This refers to giving your co-parent the first right of refusal to care for the children when the parent with whom the children most reside with is working, ill or having to leave the children for a period of time.

▶ *Major Decisions: Recreation:* Often parents share a desire for their children to be involved in recreational or artistic activities. However, opinions may differ as to what activities are best for their children: a sport may be seen as too rough; an activity may require a lot of time and commitment that may be seen to interfere with school work; or, an activity may be too cost prohibitive for a child to continue. Parents should first discuss continuing their children's participation in recreational or artistic activities they are currently enrolled in before discussing future activities. *Making every effort not to interrupt these activities will help children to feel anchored by having a routine they have come to know.* Discussion of future activities can be approached from a number of ways: initially, as parents you may already have an idea from what your children have expressed they would like to do to be able to discontinue one activity and enroll them in a program you know they have wanted to be involved in; or, you may set up a contingency plan for enrolling them in one or two activities you believe they may enjoy with the proviso the children are asked for their feedback to make a choice; and for future decisions parents should will need to focus on activities suitable for each child, time commitment and cost, including garnering child input to decide on what activities are best for their children. *Education and Religion:* For parents whose children attend public school and do not receive any formal religious studies, discussion may center on what is the best school in the area they reside that will meet their children's needs. Parents may also share the same general spiritual frame of reference without formal attendance to church, in which case a discussion concerning formal religious schooling for their children may not become an issue. However, it is not uncommon upon separation/divorce for one parent to desire for their children to attend Sunday school. When this occurs, discussion should focus on the reason one parent believes attendance at the school is important in reference to the children's best interests. Often, this perspective is rooted in one parent's desire to have their children spiritual/morally grounded in an attempt to thwart any turmoil the children may experience from the parent's break up. This may also be true if one parent advocates for their children to attend a private or religious school.

▶ *Non-emergency health care* – Parents should agree that if one parent or both have health care plans that provide for their dependants (children), whatever parts of one or both of those plan that have that maximize benefits for their children should be continued as long as possible under the terms of the plan(s).

▶ *Resolution of Conflict:* By setting out plans and contingencies for activities and issues concerning your children you will have significantly reduced the possibility a major conflict will erupt between you and the other parent. This includes setting aside a designated time to cooperatively talk and decide about issues and plans that come up about your children – by phone, e-mail, fax or mutually agreed-upon meetings. During these times both of you shall agree to refrain from making negative remarks to each other, or to use children as messengers. Here are further ways to maintain positive communication and resolve issues:

1. Continuing parenting as partners with two households.

2. Compromise and respect your adult differences.

3. Respect the other parent and your children – avoid making derogatory or demeaning remarks about the children's other parent in their presence.

4. Set aside scheduled time to review any changes that occur to avoid the possibility of confrontation when your children are present.

5. Be open to compromise and be flexible to change – avoid being critical of or controlling of the other parent.

6. Respect the other parent's privacy and boundaries. Do not ask children questions to get information about the other parent.

7. Let your children have time with their other parent and avoid preventing your child from spending time with them because you have you have unresolved financial matters.

8. Make child-support payments on time.

9. Keep your promises and agreements to build the other parent's trust.

10. Your children have a right to a relationship with their other parent, and the other parent has a right to spend time with their children.

11. When difficulties arise between a parent and child, the other parent should allow the child and parent involved to work out their difficulties without interference.

(For details on these guidelines see 'Conflict-free Zone' in the Chapter six)

Pick your battles. Focus on what needs to happen, not on who should be responsible for it – you are. Too often people start to focus on things that may be frustrating, but in the scheme of things are quite small. For example, a jacket, or some clothes, or shoes haven't traveled with a child to the other parent. This parent may focus their attention, anger, frustration on the other parent because these items were not returned, rather than making allowances for this possibility and focusing their attention on the children's experience of having a positive time with the other parent. However if, and or, when an impasse over a major issue presents itself both parents should mutually agree to using a family mediator or family counselor trained in mediation to assist you with: resolving any outstanding issues set out in your agreement; accommodating any changes (i.e. one parent moving, illness of a child, or remarriage of a parent); and, reworking any elements of the plan to meet the needs of your children as they grow and develop. Prior to having any major issue resolved by mediation decide on who will be involved – mediator or family counselor, and how such a process will be paid.

COMMUNICATION STRATEGIES TO AVOID MISUNDERSTANDINGS

1. Keep the agenda of items you want to talk about to a realistic length (whether by phone or in-person) and set a limit on the time you wish to speak to each issue. For instance, one parent may wish to reschedule an access visit for the next two weeks – this issue may only take a few minutes, while rescheduling the entire access time will probably require a considerable amount of time set aside for your discussion. (Both each parents should know what is on the agenda beforehand and have mutually agreed to it, as well as, the amount of time set aside for the discussion.)

2. When discussion become heated each parent should listen and repeat back to the other parent what you have heard to ensure you understand the intention and meaning of what the other parent has said.

    a. *Before* raising a point, ask the other parent to just listen and not reply or interrupt until finishing what you have to say. After you have spoken, ask them to repeat what you have said, not what they think you meant.

    b.   *After* they have summarized what you have said, acknowledge what they have said, and repeat doing this until they have understood your message.

    c.   *When* you are satisfied they know what you mean, ask for a reply and summarize what they have said to ensure what you have heard is accurate.

    d.   *Practice* this process with someone you know and get along well with and who can give you feedback.

3. Refrain from dredging up the past and allow the other parent to present their point of view without jumping all over it, after all you too have your own point of view and what it to be heard.

4. Both parents should allow the other parent time for thought and enquiry on some issues. Never assume that you and the other parent will be able to resolve every issue each time you meet. And never assume because it can not be resolved at that time it is due to spite.

5. Agree to allow provisional statements or agreements that may be subject to change e.g. school or recreation activities.

6. Before closing a discussion, it is best for both parties to sum up what has been agreed upon, including the actions/steps to be taken and by whom. Also, confirm when you are going to meet next and announce any topics that either parent is aware of that should be included in the next discussion.

7. As part of the rules for discussion, mutually agree there may be times when subjects may cause one or both parents to become emotionally heated, and during such times one or both parents can

    a.   *take* a time out from the discussion, and or, move on to another topic, or

    b.   *call* an end to the discussion and reschedule it for another time. If this occurs, follow step #6 above.

These strategies are intended to enhance the communication process that needs to occur between parents and reduce the chances that emotionally charged issues will hamper your ability to be parenting partners. Doing the work and developing effective communication between yourselves will translate into positive interaction with your children.

DIFFICULTIES INITIATING PARENTING PLANS

First, dismiss the idea that a parenting plan needs to be all or nothing. A parenting plan can apply to one specific issue or event, or it can address as many issues to meet your family's needs and situation.

Second, a family or parenting plan does not have to be developed all at once. Sometimes chunking or piecing together a plan is the best way to obtain consensus, as parents have time to absorb and think about issues as they proceed. It can also be a positive means to strengthen communication, build trust and develop a rapport with the other parent. This is especially true, just after separation when emotions run high and issues pertaining to the children and separation have not been settled.

Third, sometimes issues are so emotional and difficult to deal with at the time of the initial separation that setting up an initial plan may be extremely hard. If you have asked yourself the questions discussed in chapter, the feedback and insight they have provided should allow you to arrange for access. Reasons that each parent may not wish to deal with this issue vary: from feeling shell shocked; wanting to insulate or protect the children; or, due to resentment or dislike for the other parent. However, it is in the children's best interest that as parents you arrange, at least temporarily, times your children are going to be with each parent, to reduce their feelings of insecurity about where they fit in the family and continue receiving love from each parent.

Fourth, having established setting up an initial agreement or plan, perhaps of only one or a few issues, often provides parents with the impetus of setting up further parts of a plan by reminding both parents that making such an agreement is in the best interests not only for their children but in the their best interest as parents too.

Remember to be patient and, listen to the other parent and use calm language to explain your point of view.

Finally, you may have to make and accept compromises initially in order to see your children for the reasons mentioned above, in order to allow for the opportunity to fully explore the issue of access once the initial period of separation has settled.

In most situations parents are successful in agreeing to access that is better for everyone. However, in some circumstances, these matters do not improve after a number of weeks and a parent need to resolve such issues through a mediator, family counselor, divorce coach, or as a last resort a lawyer.

IMPORTANT PRACTICES TO IMPLEMENT ONCE PARENTS AGREE TO A PLAN

▶ Put into practice the agreed upon plan a.s.a.p. to avoid delays caused from second guessing by either parent

▶ Be Punctual. Delay of plans creates further stress and disappointment in children.

▶ Be Positive. Giving off positive vibes and being positive with children about seeing their other parent will bolster their confidence of feeling wanted and loved. An established routine and pattern of going between parent's residences will reassure a child they are secure and loved.

▶ Be Cheerful. Parents should be cheerful at the door both at pick up and drop off. The easier the transitions from one parent's care to the other the easier for children to feel comfortable and adapt to two households.

▶ Be Discreet. Do not share any details about your separation/divorce concerning how you feel or think about your children's other parent. Doing so will only upset your children, as the other parent is part of them and hearing such information will directly undermine their self-worth.

▶ Be Mindful. Lessen a child's anxiousness by having them ready to go with the other parent. Have children properly dressed for the activity they are going to be doing i.e. outdoor activities require a coat etc and possibly a change of clothing if the may get dirty or wet. On overnight stays children should have another set of clothing. Children should also return with what they brought on the outing or for their overnight stay. If the other parent is not certain of the activity (perhaps due to weather) they should ask the parent for a change of clothing. When possible, overnight stays, a child's clothes should be washed and set home clean. These behaviours enhance parenting as partners.

▶ Allow for Flexibility. If a child develops a cold, or an unforeseen difficultly arises in which the child is not able to see the other parent at the scheduled time and date. Work with the parent to arrange another time and date. Sometimes, a parent may offer to the other parent to look after the child if they are sick. Some parents are o.k. with this; others do not want to move the sick child possibly causing further complications. If this is the case, do not assume the parent is trying to sabotage your time with your child. Allow for contact by phone, even briefly if the child is sick, to reassure the child their other parent is not mad at them for missing their time together. As a child grows older and develops friendships with other children and starts taking part in school activities after school hours, a parent should be flexible that outings or plans may have to change – their friends may have to be included in a plan, and or, the parent may have to accompany their child to a school activity etc. In order that such an occurrence does not occur often check the school schedule for the activity your child is enrolled in to ensure it does not cause a surprise again. If it is to do with your child making plans, then talk to them about possibly including their friends on occasional outings, and gently remind them you would like to do activities with them on your own too. If the activity on that day is going to be on going and conflicting with your time with your child then it may be a good idea to discuss an alternative plan with the other parent. Remember do not raise this issue with your child, but discuss this matter first with the other parent.

▶ Allow for Creativity and Imagination. Do activities and projects as you would in a one-parent household. In other words, allow for activities to evolve and extend over a number of visits not just limited to single access activities – grow a garden, build models, do a puzzle, read a book, etc.

▶ Do Ordinary Stuff Too and Be Yourself. Mix every special activity and treat with doing ordinary stuff i.e. grocery shopping, Dr. appointments, cooking, laundry, etc. Participating in activities such as these allows a child to see you as their parent. Despite being mundane activities children will benefit more from showing them what you really do and being with them, then simply spending time trying to special activities with them. Having children participate in doing ordinary stuff builds and shapes a rapport with your children.

▶ Be Realistic and Practical. Everyone needs down time and personal space. Learn to recognize and arrange for personal space with the other parent. It is also important that children learn to recognize and use their own initiative to entertain themselves to allow their parent rest and give themselves privacy too.

▶ Parents in Charge. Listen to children's wants and requests and deal with their needs first. As part of sharing parenting discuss with the other parent what wants and requests a child makes are realistic and financially viable. Combining information and possibly resources eliminates duplication. It will lessen the likelihood a child will be able to pressure one or both parents into giving in to their demand, and it will show to the child their parent's have a unified front in making decisions and being in charge.

Simply put, working on a plan to share parenting is best for you and your children, for no one else will understand your children as you and the other parent does, and no one else will be in a position to know and understand your children's needs except their parents. Arranging a shared parenting plan will allow both parents to be responsible for parenting, allow parents to work in their children's best interests and allow for a positive parent-child interaction and bond to be formed.

A few examples of Parenting/Family Plans are presented in chapter eight. These plans are intended for general reference, though the lay out of one of the plans can be used as a template towards developing your own parent or family plan.

Chapter Six

Extra-ordinary Issues

▶ The need for your children to maintain contact with extended family
▶ Supervised Access (Visitation)
▶ Special Circumstances: Service of Papers, Being locked out of your home, Violence/Threats
▶ How to Respond to Unique Situations

THE IMPORTANCE OF EXTENDED FAMILY

Keeping your children's routines and maintaining family supports during and after divorce will certainly help your children overcome any feelings of insecurity and uncertainty they may have as a result of their parents' separation. The loss of suddenly not being able to maintain contact with cousins, grandparents, or any special family members your children may have grown up knowing and forming relationships with can be very upsetting during such a difficult time. Interacting with extended family members enables children to feel reassured and supported that they belong to a family and that they are loved no matter their parent's differences. Therefore, it is in your children's best interest that if you have had a falling-out with your in-laws you should try to find a way to mend ties and defuse the tension before you are unable to do so for your children's sake. Parents who plan for and continue their children's interaction with extended family members provide their children with a greater chance for healing and bolstering their well-being. This is true regardless if parents are married or not.

Andrew and Heather's divorce was fairly amicable. However, it came as quite a shock to both their families and left some of them very angry towards them. Both Andrew and Heather had been made to feel like a son and daughter in each other's family prior to the divorce and both of their children were adored. Once the separation occurred Andrew was told by his father-in-law, "You are welcome in our house, but don't come too often." Heather also felt shunned by her in-laws. Both families wanted little to do with their in-law and felt protective toward their family member. As a result, the children felt isolated and confused by the reaction of their extended family, especially in not being able to play with cousins and see their grandparents.

Both parents contacted me and I meet with both of them to discuss how they could speak with each of their families to defuse the tension and allow their children to become part of the larger family again.

To alleviate any concerns you and the other parent may have about discussing issues concerning your break up between each other's extended family members and your children both parents should ask their respective relatives to refrain from discussing any such matters with your children, even if your children bring up questions. You can also ask that they not make any derogatory comments about the other parent in the children's presence or put pressure on them to side against the other parent. Make sure that your extended family understands that doing any of these behaviors would cause harm to the children they care for and love.

SUPERVISED ACCESS (VISITATION)

Access, or visitation, represents how the time with a child will be spent with each parent. The term *access* is preferred over *visitation,* which implies the child and parent are "just visiting" rather than being part of a family unit.

For most couples who separate and divorce having someone supervise your visit or access with your children will seem absurd and unnecessary. However, there are a number of reasons for an access supervisor to observe a parent–child interaction.

The reason a parent may require supervised access is: mental illness; incarceration; drug use; abuse; or, violence. Often a court will order a parent to have an access supervisor present during visits with their children for a set amount of time before the matter of whether to continue supervision or not is reviewed. In a fraction of situations supervised access has been set down as a condition by the custodial parent for the other parent to visit their children because of their suspicion and concern one or more of the reasons listed above is occurring in the other parent's life. Often, like that of the courts, the question of whether supervision should be continued or not is reviewed after a prescribed timeframe.

Supervised access may also occur temporarily because of a long absence of the other parent seeing their children. A supervisor in this case, acts as an intermediary to ensure the children feel comfortable reestablishing contact and rapport with a parent that may be unfamiliar to them.

An access supervisor should be an individual qualified to observe parent-child interactions. This could be a childcare worker, family support worker, social worker, family counselor, or another professional such as a psychologist. In any case, this person should have a background in observing parent-child interactions and have training or experience as a access supervisor. They should also work for an agency, which follows a standard of rules similar with those outlined by the Supervised Visitation Network[12].

Prior to access occurring a supervisor should first meet with both parents separately to review their role and address any conditions outlined in a court order, or concerns they have about the visits. They should arrange prior to the access time(s) to meet with the children involved to explain their role and allow the children to know who they are, so when access occurs the children do not feel a complete stranger is watching them. This will allow a supervisor to be as unobtrusive as possible during visits allowing for as 'natural' an interaction to occur between parent and child. If there are no restrictions placed on how and where access can occur visits should be allowed to occur in various locations doing various activities to also allow for as 'natural' an interaction between parent and child. An access supervisor's job is to remain within eye and ear contact and enforce any conditions stated in the court order with respect to access, and or, avoid conditions or situations that could possibly jeopardize the children's welfare. Thus, the prime role of an access supervisor is to safeguard and ensure the safety and well-being of the children being supervised. A further role, through observation is for a supervisor to be able to make an accounting of the details of the parent-child interaction and rapport.

There are (fortunately only a small percentage in the scheme of couples who separate or divorce) parents who make false allegations toward the other parent to family service agencies, police or the court system and out of safety and concern for the children supervised access is imposed on the other parent. This is abuse of the system that is to protect children's welfare as one parent uses this service as a form of retaliation, or as an act of spite against the other parent. Fortunately, as I have experienced and in every incident where parents have said they are good parents and have been wronged, observation by the supervisor of the parent-child interaction and rapport with their children has verified their claim of being a good parent. Using supervision under such circumstances places added tension and stress on children who are finding adjusting to their parent's divorce difficult already. Access supervision is a necessary service to allow children to have contact with their other parent under conditions that provide for their safety and well-being. Its purpose is not to thwart and disrupt contact and parent-child interaction at the expense the children's welfare.

---

12 *The Supervised Access Network is a non-profit corporation located in the United States which exists for the benefit of children who may not have contact without support and intervention of a neutral third party.*

See Supervised Access Network on the internet for standards and guidelines.

Some provinces and states have published access (visitation) guidelines. The following is an Access Planning List to assist you with best arranging access between you and the other parent:

- Consider the age of each child and plan according to their needs. i.e. scheduling different access times for a child of ten vs. a seventeen yr. old

- Again consider not always having children of different ages attend the same access based on closeness and attachment to each other

- Consider not always having children of different ages attend the same access based on closeness and attachment to each parent

- Set up and monitor access based on how each child is handling the separation and divorce

- Factor in how travel time to and from each parent's residence, size and age appropriate stuff each parent has to accommodate each child's need

- Factor in the location of schools and the quality of education if the children are living at each parents' residences

- The difficulties of changing schools if the children are living at each parents' residences

- The need for day care or babysitting

- The need for after-school care or activities

- Transportation to and from each residence to the schools

- The work and travel schedule of each parent

- The availability of a backup babysitter for each parent

One of the questions, as a supervisor, I am commonly asked is, "What should I tell my child when their other parent does not show up for visits when they are scheduled to do so?

The answer has two parts: what a parent can preventatively do to ensure this situation does not occur; and, what support a parent can provide to their child if this scenario occurs. If this were an infrequent and random occurrence I would contact the other parent to reinforce the need to maintain regular contact with their child. Ask them to contact you by phone to cancel the visit, and so they can speak with their children to ensure they feel thought of and loved. Let that parent know how it affects their child from feeling disappointed and sad to withdrawal and showing a temper. Let them know how important visits with their parent is to feel loved, wanted and feeling good about themselves, and by not calling or showing up can cause a child to feel abandoned and that their parent's absence is somehow their fault. If you suspect this may occur again, or you are feeling uncertain about whether visits will not be missed again I would recommend you not tell your children when the next visit with their other parent is going to take place until the evening before or the morning of the day a visit is to occur. If this is an on-going problem, speak to the parent as described above, and if no steps are taken by that parent to correct the situation, it may be in your child's best interest to temporarily suspend access until you are reassured by that parent that visits will be regular, and or, consistent.

In dealing at the time, with your child's feelings empathize with her disappointment while supporting their love of that parent. For example, "[Child's name], I know how much you were looking forward to seeing Mom/Dad and it is ok to feel disappointed that they are not coming to see you. I would be too if I were you. I know they love you very much. Sometimes things happen that we do not know about before they happen and it does not allow us to do things we want to do. When you feel a little better, let me know, and maybe we can do something else. I am going to be… I love you." Do not try to "cheer up" your child and do not make any disparaging remarks about that parent. Also, encourage them to talk to their other parent about how they feel when they are let down by not having a visit.

Children of any age need consistency regarding access. Establishing a pattern of spending consistent and regular times with your children allows them to adjust, feel secure and develop a sense of stability about what is going on in the 'present' family.

SPECIAL CIRCUMSTANCES: SERVICE OF PAPERS, BEING LOCKED OUT OF YOUR HOME, VIOLENCE/THREATS/INTIMIDATION
SERVICE OF PAPERS

In the event you are served divorce papers take notice that you have thirty days from the date served to respond. You should consult a lawyer, preferably a family law lawyer, as soon as possible and get them fully explain what the papers mean and what options are concerning the divorce process. If you have been served with papers concerning a temporary restraining order, contact a lawyer immediately, as the time to reply to this document may be shorter.

BEING LOCKED OUT OF YOUR HOME OR MATRIMONIAL RESIDENCE

What should you do if you find yourself locked out of your home? It is in your best interest, and that of your children, not to make a spectacle outside the residence. Try to stay calm and focus on the task, which is to resolve the situation of getting into the home in as peaceful manner as possible. Try to contact your spouse or partner, or have a mutual friend contact them to enquire as to their intentions of locking you out of the home. Next, consult with a lawyer, or visit your local police station to find out whether your spouse has the legal right to keep you out of the residence, such as a valid restraining order allowing them sole access of the home. If so, get a copy of the order. Finally, consult a family law lawyer about rescinding the order if there is one, or about getting a valid restraining order against your spouse placing you back in the home and forcing them to vacate the home. If you believe this matter may escalate, consult with your lawyer about having the locks changed to prevent any future commotion from your spouse.

VIOLENCE/THREATS/INTIMIDATION

If you have been the victim of violence, physical or otherwise, threatened or intimidated by your partner or spouse, live in fear for yourself, and or your children you will need to do one of two behaviors. First, in either case, you will have to make a decision and a commitment to yourself that the situation you find yourself will end. Then, you will need to either make a plan about how you and your children will remove yourselves from the home and the abuser, or you develop a strategy with a lawyer to legally ensure and require your spouse leaves the home and is legally served with papers to have no contact with you, and or, your children.

Many people see their situation as hopeless, believing even if they did leave they could not afford to care for themselves, and or, their children. However, part of the plan before you leave is to find out what friends, social service agencies and community groups will be able to assist with rent or shelter, food, and clothing.

Some of you may feel embarrassed seeking help from family or from outside sources having to expose your problem, or out of a feeling you are imposing on them. However, if you make plan and keep in mind taking such action is only temporary and pale compared to continuing to live a life in the shadow of fear and violence, then this should motivate you to continue to move forward towards a better life.

If leaving is not an option, then taking legal means is the only choice left. Consult with a lawyer what process can be taken to ensure your safety and that of your children. In most states and provinces a spouse or partner can be charged with assault and battery. Prior to hearing the charges you – your lawyer, can request that your spouse be kept in jail pending a hearing, and that if bail is granted you be given police protection awaiting the hearing. In some states and provinces there are even special laws to deal with family violence. These laws allow you to have your spouse removed from the home without resorting to having them thrown in jail.

When in doubt about what plan of action to take consult a lawyer to discuss which option and plan of action is best for you and your family.

HOW TO RESPOND TO UNIQUE SITUATIONS

WHEN ONE PARENT USES THEIR CHILDREN TO UNDERMINE THE OTHER PARENT'S CREDIBILITY

Some parents, feeling hurt, angry or betrayed by the other parent use their children as a means of retaliating and punishing the other parent. They will attempt to manipulate the children's time and activities so little time can be spent with the other parent, while at the same time try to undermine their credibility by discussing half-truths, stories and lies about the other parent's life. If you suspect or know this occurs it is best to avoid doing the same behavior in response. If you can talk to this parent about how this behavior can affect your children. Emphasize that they love and need both of you and that saying-disparaging remarks makes them question their own feeling and harms their sense of self-worth. If they refuse to listen – which is often the case – it may be necessary to enlist the help of a counselor or divorce coach – someone who could deliver the same message but be viewed as a neutral third party. Most often if you stay consistent with your behavior (actions speak louder than words) you will find in time your children will figure out where the truth lies and if their actions continue the children will come to resent that parent for behaving in such a manner.

WHAT IF A PARENT NEVER HAS THE CHILDREN READY ON TIME, OR NEVER RETURNS THE CHILDREN ON THE AGREED-ON TIME?

First, discuss the issue with the other parent. Do not jump to conclusions that the other parent is doing it to frustrate you. More often than not I have observed in my practice that simple adjustments in scheduling can rectify problems and alleviate stress. For example, a couple I met needed to resolve the issue of one parent who arrived to pick up the children at the scheduled time often found the children were usually not ready and sometimes activities that had been planned for i.e. going to the movies caused them to be late. We looked at what was going on prior to scheduled visits and found that on weekdays the children often felt rushed and needed more time to do homework before their visit time. On weekends, the children needed more time to do their weekly chores. A simple reworking of access times eliminated the problem regarding the parent having to wait during pick up.

If you are not able to contact the other parent directly to resolve this issue you may have to a) go to court to vary access to ensure you are able to do scheduled activities with your children, b) contact them via letter, and or, their lawyer, without being derogatory, state that your X hour scheduled visit will begin from the time the children leave the house and not at the appointed time. I am sure you will receive a call or letter back from their lawyer – it is a starting point to resolve the issue.

The same process can be used to figure out the reason for one parent often returning the children later than the scheduled time. Does that parent consistently return the children x, y, z time after each visit, or does it vary? Are the children doing an activity, such as homework that they are completing before they return to the other parent? When the children are late, are they visiting grandparents or other relatives, which requires more travel time to get to and from where they live?

Once you have the answers to these questions you will be able to figure out what solutions may be possible to resolve this issue. Be flexible and be willing to compromise for the sake of your children. Before any changes occur briefly tell the children about then so they are prepared when the changes occur.

A COMMON QUESTION, ASKED OUT OF CONCERN IN ANTICIPATING SUCH AN EVENT, IS WHAT SHOULD I DO IF MY FORMER SPOUSE OR PARTNER STARTS TO MAKE A SCENE IN FRONT OF THE CHILDREN?

Remember this: It takes only one parent to start a scene, but it takes two to keep it going. Therefore, the best behavior you can do is to disengage – if they shout, remain calm and keep your normal tone of voice. If they continue, you continue to talk calmly and with a normal voice. You do not need to respond to each comment they raise. Simply state, "This is not the time nor the place to discuss this and I will not discuss this here and now in front of the children." Complete the child exchange, give any pertinent information about the children to the other parent and leave.

WHAT DO YOU DO IF YOU HAVE NOTICED AN APPARENT CHANGE IN HOW YOUR CHILD BEHAVES TOWARDS YOU AND OTHERS? WHAT IF THEY SEEM TO BE WITHDRAWING INTO THEMSELVES? WHAT IF THEY ARE ACTING OUT?

In both situations it is best that a parent talk with their child to find out what is going on for the child and to ask how the separation, and or, divorce is affecting them. A common occurrence by parents is to insulate their child from feeling pain about the lose of their family, because they themselves feel defensive and guilty for burdening their child with having to experience divorce. However, it is best for a parent to acknowledge and be supportive of their child to express their feelings. Tell them both their parents love them and that what happened between their parents was not because of anything they did. If a child cannot feel comfortable or has no means to do so, children may vent their feelings in the form of anger towards others or withdraw inside themselves. If a child does not want to talk do not force them, as this may further alienate them, but reassure them that you are there to listen when they are ready to talk.

WHAT HAPPENS WHEN THE OTHER PARENT HAS CUSTODY OF THE CHILDREN AND THE CHILDREN ARE RESISTIVE TO SPENDING TIME WITH YOU? WHAT SHOULD YOU DO?

This is a scenario I see occurring with a few families each year. What typically is happening is that the custodial parent is still stuck and has not moved past resolving their feelings toward you, and is consciously manipulating or unwittingly causing the children to not want to see their other parent. When asked, children have even said they did not want to see their other parent, but do not volunteer a reason for not wanting to go. Since the children live with the custodial parent, and depend on them for their day-to-day security and sense of belonging children will not usually say anything to upset this arrangement, and a custodial parent will take advantage of this.

Regardless of this, you should insist on having the children. As I have witnessed, once children go with the other parent on a visit and are away from the influence of the custodial parent, children often warm up and positively interact with their other parent. Often talking to the other parent is of little use, however sometimes encouraging them to seek counseling has helped. If the situation deteriorates further to the point where your children, and or, former partner refuses on their behalf to see you, you may have to return to court to enforce the order. Be prepared that this matter can drag on for a long time. Regardless of situation, continue to write letters, send e-mails, cards etc. to your children so they know you love and care for them. If you suspect they are not getting this stuff. Ask and enlist the help of a mutual friend to ensure this stuff gets to your children, but do not jeopardize your relationship with them by pressuring them into acting as a go between if they feel too uncomfortable about doing this.

WHEN SHOULD I, AS A PARENT, SEEK HELP FOR MY CHILDREN FROM A PROFESSIONAL?

As you observe your children's reactions to separation and divorce, it is important not to be on the lookout for the worst. If you are constantly watching over your children, anticipating problems to occur, chances are good you will find them, and quite possibly may even cause them. When children appear to be struggling with adjusting to the separation and divorce, remember this is normal, and with support, encouragement, and nurturing from both parents most children adjust very well in time to their family's new circumstance. The key word here is time, so parent's need to be patient and allow their children to adjust according to meting their own needs and their own timetable.

It is normal and healthy, for example, for children with divorced parents to miss the absent parent and long for the family the way it was prior to the divorce. They may also pretend that the absent parent is there, or dream about the family being 'whole' again. Allowing and encouraging children to talk about memories and express their feelings are positive outlets for children to deal with the pain and sadness they feel about no longer being a 'whole' family. Parents should participate in these discussions talking about positive times of being a family and slowly introduce positive aspects of being a family, as it exists now. They should be careful not to disparage the other children's parent and take care to not cause their children to feel "bad" for discussing such thoughts and wishes.

You should seek professional help if this, or any other issues listed below, persist for six months or longer, depending on the specific issue. Here are some indicators you need to seek a professional's help:

- There is a noticeable change in behavior currently vs. prior to the separation i.e. crying a lot, pre-occupied with worry, angry vs. having been upbeat.
- School performance declines noticeably following the separation, and remains poor with no evidence of learning or social problems.
- School performance greatly improves at the expense of all other activities, including socializing with peers and friends.
- The child develops fears and phobias that seem unreasonable and interfere with normal activities.
- The child's play continues to focus on the family breakup or getting back together.
- The child's optimism turns to discussion about death and dying; they continue to show signs of low self-esteem, low self-confidence; or they withdraw/isolate themselves from other people.
- Their sleeping pattern continues to be disrupted – inability to sleep; sleep too much; sleeping on parent's bed; nightmares, and or, night terrors.
- The child takes on a pseudo-adult role and loses interest in doing age appropriate activities.
- The child begins to act in a provocative sexual manner.

Having one or two of these behaviors should not necessarily be cause for alarm.

However, if the behavior coincides with an abrupt or dramatic change in behavior from what seems normal; a group of behaviors become apparent; or, they persist for more than six months are signals professional intervention may be needed.

If a child talks about suicide; mutilates themselves; kills animals; adopts ritualistic behaviors like lining up toys before bed, or setting their place at the table the same way etc.; or lashes out at people in anger or physically bullies people you should seek immediate professional help.

When going to see a counselor or therapist ensure they specialize in the treatment of children and are aware of behaviors associated with separation and divorce.

Chapter Seven

Blended and Non-Traditional Families

▶ Blended Families
▶ Non-Traditional Families

BLENDED FAMILIES

There are a number of variations that arise when examining blended families which the following comments address: a single adult marries, and or, moves in with a Mom or Dad who has children: parents from previous relationships marry, and or, live together bringing together their children; a parent from a previous relationship marries, and or, lives with another Mom or Dad who has children, and they have access to their children. Going blindly into any of these scenarios, if you are the person entering into another family, without first recognizing your boundaries and role is a recipe for disaster. It is very important for a person in such a position to be aware that you will now take on a role of parenting your partner's children, and that you being part of this blended family take on challenges of dealing with the children's entire family.

During an initial period of adjustment having established your blended family it is best that you support the other parent's parenting rather than imposing your own parenting style onto your partner's children. Doing so will assist you and the children to establish a parent-child role and avoid putting you and the children at odds with each other – not to say this won't happen, you will lessen the frequency and likelihood such tension will arise. Children will find it difficult to protest if you are supporting a direction they know comes from their parent. If you are finding it difficult to support certain parenting practices of your partner, follow through with supporting what the other parent has instructed the children to do at that moment and discuss this issue with them away from the children so as to always demonstrate a united front to the children. Repeat this practice until you and the other parent have come to a resolution – this may mean you stay the course with the original practice, or you present any changes together to the children to eliminate any he said she said scenarios from happening.

The best parenting tools you can use to assist your blended children is patience and understanding. Applying these skills will allow you and your partner to develop a stronger relationship. Patience may be required if the children are having a difficult time struggling with feelings of being disloyal to their other parent and will resist bonding with you. In some situations, as I have witnessed, children feel pressured by the other parent not to accept you as they portray you as being responsible for taking their parent away from them. Whatever the circumstance, step back from the situation, be patient and assess what options you can best take before acting, especially when problems seem to be overwhelming. The more you can reduce conflict between you and your blended family, between your partner and the other parent, the better your relationship will be between you, your blended children and their parent, and the happier your relationship will be with your partner.

Dave was a single man who had been in relationships involving children before his relationship to June and her two children, Matthew and Anne. Therefore, it came as no surprise to Dave that he and June dated for almost six months before he met the children. June told the children about Dave a few weeks after they began seeing one another. Once their relationship began to become serious and prior to Dave meeting the children, they talked about some of the possible difficulties he may face parenting her children. Both agreed it was best for him to be supportive of her parenting and differ any questions he had on issues to her to avoid problems.

Both the children and Dave got along well prior to their mother's marriage to Dave. However, he observed a few times when the children treated their mother poorly and he wanted to step in. Life as a blended family for a few months was pleasant and Dave's rapport with the children seemed positive. Dave however witnessed how both children treated their Mom while shopping for clothes for the upcoming school year. He had mentioned his displeasure at seeing the children pressure her into buying clothes for them. She said she appreciated the support but she felt comfortable in dealing with the children. A month or so later the children began to get anxious about buying clothes for the spring and began hounding their Mom to go shopping for clothes and for money to buy accessories. Each time they pressured their Mom to get things they wanted and heard her say no the more demanding and disrespectful they seem to become from Dave's perspective. He was at the point where if that happened again he could not take a 'back seat' to watching June get attacked like that. A few days later, the children began pressuring their Mom, enough was enough, and Dave intervened.

Soon voices were raised, the children told Dave he wasn't their father and they wouldn't do what he told them to do. June was placed in the middle and no matter what she did, her children and Dave would not see her as being supportive or caring towards them. She asked Dave to keep quiet and leave the room for the moment and she would talk to him after she had talked with the children. She told the children she agreed with Dave that they were being pushy towards her and that she felt he intervened because he did not see them listening to what she (June) had been saying. She also said they said some very hurtful comments to Dave who had shown only care and love towards them and did not deserve the comments they had said to him.

The children, at first, held fast that they felt he had no right in interfering and that their mother was taking his side. However, after talking to them about his being part of the family, acknowledging that despite Dave not being their father that he will be parenting and making household decisions with her the children acknowledged that they had said some hurtful comments to Dave and would apologize to him. June talked to Dave and acknowledged his support however, she said that the matter was being handled and that he did not need to have defended her in that way. She felt he should have talked to her before charging in. He too, at first, defended the actions he took, saying the children seemed way over the top in pressuring her to get clothes for them. However, after discussing what had happened he realized had he spoken to June about how he felt about her being pressured to find out if this was the case, he would have found out that typically the children behaved like this only to calm down once they knew their mother would not budge on her position. The best rule is not to assume what is going on for the other parent, but discuss your perception and feeling about parenting issues with the other parent. You will often get an accurate description of what is occurring for that parent, you can then find out how to best support that parent and not make a situation worse by taking action on your own.

A family meeting was called, the children apologized to Dave for their comments and Dave reaffirmed what their mother had said to them. June confirmed what he had said and the children acknowledged Dave as a member of their family and a parent to them.

Alan, a parent from a previous relationship, remarried Kathy. Both are parents of two children. Alan's children reside with their mother and Kathy's children live with Alan and Kathy. Alan developed a positive rapport with both of her children, however as the months past since they married he felt more and more pressure to spend time with his own children. He began spending more free time with his own children to make up for the time he spent getting to know Kathy and her children after and prior to the marriage. Kathy at first felt this was fine considering he had spent a considerable amount of time with them and needed to reacquaint himself with them and them with him. Alan's former partner was cooperative with Alan seeing the children at first, however she began to resent his infringing upon her time and the children's to satisfy his desire to be with them. In return for seeing the children, she began to put conditions onto the visits, such as, that he fix the stairs that needed repairing; hook up the washer and dryer, and clean up the yard.

Alan soon began spending more and more of his free time doing chores at her home and spending time with his children than with Kathy and his other family.

Kathy spoke to Alan about his behavior. She mentioned that he was spending far too much time with his former partner and children. Alan reacted to her comments with, "so my children are not as important as yours..." Thus began nearly two weeks of tension where Alan went through the motion of putting time in with Kathy and the children before leaving to see his children. Finally, Alan and Kathy spoke at great length about what had happened, how she was feeling and how Alan thought about what was best for him and the family.

Any kind of friction caused by placing a natural parent in a position of having to choose between their natural children verses the other parent, and or, their children will result in a power struggle. Even if the other parent is 'right' the situation will usually result in the natural parent and children bonding together to form a united front against the other parent. In situations like Alan's and Kathy's it is best that you discuss and decide on a plan before rushing into action, and if or as problems arise discuss them before they get out of control. If it had been Alan's children (Kathy's stepchildren), who pressed for more time with their parent the same process should occur to avoid any frustration concerning expectation of time they should be spending in the new family.

A common occurrence when families breakup, and then form blended families is for one, sometimes both parents, to spend less time with their children now they are in a new family situation with children from the new relationship. Often that parent, or both parents, do not realize the hurt and rejection their children are feeling being shunned by someone who is supposes to care and love them. If it is one parent try to talk to them about how their child is feeling about not seeing that parent. If they refuse suggest counseling, and consider taking your child to a counselor to deal with their rejection by that parent. Continue to send pictures and information about the child's school progress and activities to this parent. I have often seen in such situations a parent or children take the initiative to reunite after an absence.

NON – TRADITIONAL FAMILIES

- *Common-Law Relationships*
- Same-Sex Relationships

The concept of family has changed in North America and around the world. In non-traditional family laws to protect all members of the family are now in certain jurisdictions being legally included in what is recognized as family. If your relationship is ending having lived in a non-traditional relationship there are a few things you need to know about your circumstances and how the laws recognize your circumstances.

COMMON-LAW RELATIONSHIPS

It is estimated there are as many common-law unions as marriages. In addition, about 40 percent of common-law couples are raising children. Unfortunately, statistics also show that there is considerably less stability in a common-law family than a marriage – up to 70 percent of these relationships end in separation within the first five years.

There are seven general factors in determining whether the law in your jurisdiction views your common-law relationship as a married couple. They are:

1. Shelter – does the unmarried couple share accommodation;

2. Sexual & Personal Behavior – does the couple have an intimate and interpersonal relationship;

3. Services – does the couple share the traditional function as a family;

4. Social – does the married couple portray themselves as a married couple in public;

5. Societal – how are the common-law couple treated by the community;

6. Economic Support – are the unmarried couple interdependent; and

7. Children – does the unmarried couple see the children as part of their home and interact parentally with each other's children.

If you and your partner have been living together for a certain number of years[13], or if you have had a child together, family law recognizes you as a married couple and you have the right to ask for support. However, in Canada, you must request spousal support within two years of the end of your relationship.

Of note, many jurisdictions in Canada and the United States have their own definition of a common-law relationship. While a general definition is "two people who have cohabited in a conjugal relationship for a period of time, or are the natural or adoptive parents of a child," the actual timeframe differs based on the law of the jurisdiction you reside. Since people who have cohabited for just one year are considered common-law under tax codes in both countries, they can claim each other as dependents and contribute to pension plans for each other.

---

13 In Ontario and New Brunswick it is 3 years, and in British Columbia and Nova Scotia it is 2 years. There are fifteen states and the District of Columbia that recognize common law as marriage immediately by telling the community you are married, through the use of the same last name, and filing of joint income tax. They are: Alabama, Colorado, Ohio, Georgia, Idaho, Iowa, Kansas, Montana, New Hampshire, Oklahoma, Pennsylvania, Rhode Island, South Carolina, Texas and Utah.

In the United States, the break up of a common-law relationship is treated the same as if it were a marriage breakup.

In Canada, a number of similarities in law exist between common-law and married. Two areas of particular interest to the reader would be Child Support as well as, Custody – determined based on what is in the child's best interest, both treated the same as marriage under the law. However, there are a few differences to be aware of: division of property; division of the house you as a couple resided in; and in order to claim for support you must file within two years of your separation.

Be aware each person is responsible for their own debts, except both are responsible for household debts such as rent and for your partner's tax liabilities.

If in doubt about any issue pertaining to your rights and those of your children it is best you find out in your jurisdiction the position taken toward common-law by first seeking counsel from a family justice agency or by getting advise from a lawyer. Once you find answers to your questions, decide on how you wish to proceed. This may depend upon whether you live in a jurisdiction that recognizes common-law as being married or not; whether your partner and you have an amiable relationship; and, how you see issues regarding child access, alimony, and child support being resolved. With any or all of these issues a mediator, divorce coach, and or, a lawyer may be of assistance in dealing with each issue.

SAME-SEX RELATIONSHIPS

In the United States, recognition of same-sex unions as being legally married only occurs in Massachusetts. In a few other states, such as Connecticut, California, New Jersey and Maine same-sex couples have varying degrees of limited legal protection. In addition, the states of Vermont and Hawaii recognize same-sex couples obtain many legal rights as married couples through the registered partnership model. If you live in any of these states, I would suggest you contact the county courthouse or Attorney General's department nearest you to obtain guidelines concerning your rights.

In Canada, the Supreme Court of Canada, in May of 1999, declared that same-sex couples are no different from heterosexual couples in their ability to share loving unions and suffer when those relationships fail. Three provinces – Quebec, Nova Scotia and Manitoba have all passed legislation to allow same-sex couples to record their relationships in a civil registry, equivalent to common-law relationships. In Alberta and British Columbia, there have been changes in several laws to recognize spousal benefits and adoption. I would suggest you contact the provincial courts or Ministry of the Attorney General office nearest you to obtain information concerning your rights.

Chapter Eight

Appendices

▶ Separation and Divorce Tips
▶ Examples of Parenting/Family Plans
▶ Creating a Conflict-free Environment for Children

SEPARATION AND DIVORCE TIPS

1. Keep your emotions in check and do not allow them to get away on you so that you can make better decisions.

2. Use friends and family for support, but use their words cautiously because they can easily 'muddy the water' that appeared clear before the advice.

3. Set your own goals and keep them realistic.

4. Try to be open, flexible, and be prepared to compromise on issues to move through the divorce to prevent unnecessary impasses from occurring. Being unwilling to move forward will cause undue stress to you and your children.

5. Do not making disparaging or derogatory comments to or about the other partner, and keep the lines of communication open so you can negotiate on issues as they arise without having to involve costly legal bills.

6. A negotiated settlement between yourself and the other person lasts as long as both of you want it to last, whereas a court imposed settle only lasts until another issue needs to be resolved.

7. Fighting for the sake of fighting creates and perpetuates a lasting war of emotional turmoil with adverse financial costs.

8. Once in court both parties give up deciding issues for themselves.

9. Never sign an agreement without fully understanding want is in the agreement, and without first seeing a lawyer.

10. Ultimately, the only person we have control over is our self, and the only behaviour we can manage is our own.

11. Working together on a parenting plan to establish ground rules, allows parents' interaction to evolve into a positive business relationship of parenting partners.

SAMPLE. PARENTING PLAN #1

1. The parents have agreed on, 20_____, that they are committed to the plan set forth below, with the goal of more shared decision-making on educational, medical, development and counseling issues.

2. They plan to communicate on a regular basis regarding the need and welfare of their children_____, so that he/she/they do not have to relay or communicate information, nor feel responsible for any miscommunication or understanding that may arise.

3. They agree to accept and not interfere with the differences that are in each home.

4. The parents shall jointly choose all schools, health-care providers, and counselors.

5. Each parent is empowered to obtain emergency health care for child/children without the consent of the other. Each parent is to notify the other parent as soon as possible if an illness or injury requires a physician's care. All matters for surgery or dental work shall be discussed and resolved before the work commences.

6. Should either parent need to be absent from the home overnight while is/are in his/her custody, the other parent should be advised and given the opportunity to care for her/him/them before other arrangements are made.

7. If the opportunity is taken advantage of, the other parent agrees to an equal exchange at his/her convenience with_____in months of the arrangement.

8. Each parent will provide the other with the address and telephone number of -_____'s residence while with him/her. Reasonable notice will be provided for any anticipated travel, and itinerary be provided.

9. Each parent shall be entitled to reasonable telephone communication with. Each parent will respect their child's/child right to privacy during such telephone conversations.

10. The parents will share custody of their child/children according to following physical custody plan:

A. HOLIDAYS AND SPECIAL DAYS

- DayEven Years Odd Years
- Memorial Day
- July 4th Weekend
- Labor Day
- Thanksgiving Vacation
- Father's Day Weekend
- Mother's Day Weekend
- Christmas Vacation
- Winter Vacation
- Spring Vacation
- Other DAYS deemed important

B THREE-DAY WEEKENDS

Each year's three-day weekends shall be divided equally between each home. The parent's will meet at the beginning of the school year and prior to the final three months of the school year to review the year's balance, and make any needed adjustment if an imbalance exits.

C. SUMMER SCHOOL VACATION

Same as basic schedule except for family vacation trips on an exchange basis and agreed upon by. Mother's preference in Father's preference in

D. BASIC SCHEDULE

Child's name_____ Days_____

Child's name_____ Days_____

Child's name_____ Days_____

Whenever a school or legal holiday falls upon the Friday preceding or the Monday following a weekend, the parent who has physical custody for the weekend shall also have physical custody on the holiday.

E. THE PARENTS WILL COMMUNICATE ON A REGULAR BASIS AS FOLLOWS:

    a. *Blocks* of time to be resolved by 30 days prior to the start of each calendar year

     b. *Other* communication to be written and mailed and, if necessary, the matters to be discussed over the phone.

11. Each parent shall be responsible for keeping himself/herself advised of all school, athletic, or social events in which_____ participate(s). Each parent will be responsible for arranging for *joint* meetings with their child's/children's individual teachers, whether requested by the parent or the teacher. Major school activities and all matters with school/parent communications should be shared.

12. Except as otherwise agreed between the parents, each parent pick up the child/children at the beginning of each of his or her custody periods.

13. In the event that a decision cannot be made jointly by us, we propose to submit the differences to:for mediation services.

14. Each parent will at all times exert every effort to maintain free and unhampered contact between_____and his/her/their parent and agree to foster a feeling of affection between his/her/other parent. Neither parent will do anything to estrange_____ from the other parent or which would distort his/her/their opinion of their father or mother or would impair his/her/their *love* and *respect* for each of them.

15. Our intention in order to promote optimal continuity and stability for _____ is to remain within (insert geographical area or school district).

Dated: _____   Signed:_____

Dated: _____   Signed:_____

SAMPLE. PARENTING PLAN #2

We,_____and_____ the mother and father of
_____ and _____ born have developed the following plan in order to insure____ and _____'s optimal development. We wish to set forth what we can reasonably expect of the other parent. We wish to provide continuity, stability, and predictability for___ and ___, while insuring that they will have frequent and continuing contact with each of their parents.

I. JOINT DECISION-MAKING

We agree to jointly make all major decisions regarding _____ and _____'s education, health, and general welfare. We agree that all day-to-day decisions will be made individually.

II. INFORMATION EXCHANGE

We agree to exchange information regarding all of _____ and _____'s activities, including but not limited to health, education, general welfare, and activities. We are in agreement that this should be done in a manner that is not intrusive on the other parent's personal life.

III. MEDICAL EMERGENCIES

We agree that if____ requires emergency medical or dental care, the parent each child is with will secure the necessary services and inform the other parent as soon as possible.

IV. BASIC SCHEDULE

We agree to the following basic schedule:
Monday-Wednesday-Mother
Tuesday-Thursday-Father
Friday-alternate between parents
Weekends-Split
When a parent cannot be with -_____ during his/her time of responsibility, adequate notice will be given of that fact.
Adequate notice is considered _____.

V. HOLIDAYS, SPECIAL DAYS, HOLY DAYS, THREE-DAY WEEKENDS, CHRISTMAS, EASTER, PASSOVER, CHANUKAH, ROSH HASHANA

We agree that _____will be with their_____- for days during Christmas. For Easter, we agree that will be with their_____for_____days. We agree to alternate the following three-day weekends: Martin Luther King, Jr. Day; Presidents' Day; Memorial Day; Fourth of July and Labour Day.

We agree to alternate Thanksgiving between odd and even years.

We agree both parents are entitled to vacation with each child, and each parent shall give notification to the other parent in a timely fashion and mutually agree to decide upon dates.

During the summer, the basic schedule will prevail unless other plans have been arranged.

Other special days to be planned include: Mother's/Father's Day, Father's, Mother's and relatives birthdays

VI.COMMUNICATION

We agree to arrange a time and day when we can discuss parental issues. We shall use e-mail or telephone on the day and time arranged to discuss only matters concerning our parent/children issues.

VII.RESPECTING EACH OTHER

Both parents shall be mindful and respectful towards each other in the presence of their children.

VIII.FIRST REFUSAL BY EACH PARENT TO PROVIDE CARE

If the parent who is caring for the children is unable during their parental caregiving to care and provide for the needs of the children, due to illness, emergency or extraordinary circumstances, the other parent has first refusal to provide care for the children before another party, such as a relative or friend is contacted to provide intervening care.

IX.PROVISION FOR SCHEDULED TIME

The parents agree that in the event such an occurrence happens and lasts more than _____ days the absent parent will have the opportunity to make up the scheduled time with the children.

X.MEDIATION

Both parents agree that if life changes of one or both parents, or changes in the lives of their children precipitate changes to the agreement, either or both parents can request and return to mediation to mutually update, and or, to resolve any issues before taking the matter to court.

Dated: _____   Signed:_____

Dated: _____   Signed:_____

CREATING A CONFLICT-FREE ENVIRONMENT FOR CHILDREN

Guidelines for treating each other as parenting partners.

1. *Shift thinking from <u>solely seeing the person as the 'ex'</u> to being a parenting partner.* Focus on your children's needs and not on the regrets and breakdown of the relationship.

2. Discuss changes in scheduling, parenting issues etc. by taking a step back and looking at the situation before deciding – *show respect to the other's ideas and differences in opinion; compromise; and settle any disagreements through give-and-take.*

3. *Show civility and respect to your children by treating the other parent with courtesy and respect* by demonstrating a pleasant environment when the other parent is around and speaking to them without making derogatory comments about them in the presence of the children.

4. When you are upset or feeling confrontational, or you find the other parent is angry or wanting to be confrontational it is in the CHILDREN'S BEST IN-TEREST to *discuss only matters pertaining to children's issues.*

5. If you have an immediate concern quietly pull the other parent aside to discuss an issue of importance i.e. child's health, safety or welfare – out of child's hearing. *Do not be overly critical or dominating towards the other parent* so they do not become defensive and resist listening to your concern. Let the small concerns i.e. a parent being late pass and raise the issue when you next speak with them.

6. *Respect the other parent's privacy and avoid discussing your desire to reconcile your relationship.* If the other parent is willing to discuss such matters do so away from the children and seek counseling to avoid traumatizing the

children if you do not reconcile. If the other parent is not willing to discuss the matter, pursuing the issue can spill over and result in a child feeling frustrated being reminded that their family has changed.

7. *Discuss money issues away from children and do not use children as bargaining tools to reach a financial settlement*

8. *For the benefit of your child make your child-support payments on time.* Again, if you and your parenting partner are having difficulty over financial matters do not use your children as bargaining tools. It only exacerbates matters rather than helps to resolve them.

9. *Build the other parent's trust by fulfilling commitments, meeting schedules and keeping agreements.*

10. *Allow your children the right to develop a bond and rapport with the other parent and the other parent the opportunity to spend time with them.*

11. *When difficulties arise between a parent and child, the other parent should allow the child and parent involved to work out their difficulties without interference (except if it involves the child's safety or welfare).*

References

Ahrons, Constance R. The Good Divorce. New York. Harper Collins, 1994.

Ahrons, Constance R. We're Still Family. New York. Harper Collins, 2003.

Anderson, Keith. OnYour Own Again. Toronto. McClelland & Stewart, 1995.

Bienenfield, Florence. Helping Your Child Through Your Divorce. 2nd revised ed.

Alameda, Ca. Hunter House, 1987.

Burrett, Jill F. Dad's Place: a new guide for fathers after divorce. Sydney, Aust.

Harper Collins, 1996.

Everett, Craig A. Healthy Divorce. San Francisco. Jossey-Bass, 1994.

Kubler-Ross, Elizabeth. Death and Dying. 3rd ed. New York. Touchstone, 1991

Marquardt, Elizabeth. Between Two Worlds: The Inners Lives of Children of Divorce. New York. Three Rivers Press, 2006.

Robertson, Christina. A Woman's Guide to Divorce and Decision Making:

A Supportive Workbook for Women Facing the Procees of Divorce. 2nd ed. New York. Simon & Schuster, 1988.

Vaz-Oxlade, Gail E. Divorce: A Canadian Woman's Guide. Toronto. Prentice Hall, 2000.

Belli, Melvin M. and Mel Krantzler. Divorcing. New York. St. Martin's Press, 1988.

Benedek, Elissa P. and Catherine F. Brown. How to Help Your Child Overcome Your Divorce. WASHINGTON, D.C. American Psychiatric Press, 1995.

Overrington, Caroline. A story online distributed by *The Australian News* on a study By Dr. Jenn McIntosh for the Institute of Family Studies. October 2006

Index